WHEEL PATTER

MEMOIRS OF IRISH MOTOR SPORT

By

DUDLEY COLLEY

with a Foreword by
STANLEY WOODS

and an introduction by
WILFORD FITZSIMMONS

An additional chapter by
TONY COLLEY

with an introduction by
DAVID DUNN

Published by
LOFT PUBLICATIONS
Kilmatead, Clondalkin, Dublin 22. Ireland.
www.wheelpatter.com

Published May 2003

ISBN 0-9544842-0-7

Set in 12pt on 13pt Palatino
Typesetting by Links Publications
Printed on 115gsm Chromomatt
Printed and bound by Betaprint

To those who regard
the motor vehicle as a friend and partner
rather than as a means
of transport

Dudley Colley 1911 - 1959

INTRODUCTION

WHEN Dudley Colley paid me the compliment of asking me to write an introduction to his book, I, as a man who for the greater part of my life have done my racing on two wheels, felt that I would be biting off rather a large slice in attempting to introduce a book mainly concerned with motor cars and car racing. However, when I read Dudley's book in manuscript form, I began to see very clearly how similar are the joys and pains of all those who take an active part in what we enthusiasts call " The Sport ". Let it be trials, races, or what you will, enthusiasm is the keynote to success.

Very often this enthusiasm is mistaken for a mild form of madness which assails young men in their teens and gradually passes off when the so-called age of reason is reached. Nothing could be further from the truth. The vast majority of competitors in all forms of the sport do their own tuning and preparation for the events in which they intend to compete. They spend the major part of their spare time in the pursuit of perfection, both in their own skill in riding or driving, and in the careful and sometimes highly technical preparation of their machines. There are those who through lack of cash or mechanical knowledge cannot hope for any great success, and after hours of toil meet very often with the bitter disappointment of mechanical failure at the last moment; but they are not down-hearted, and they keep coming back for more.

There are those who from the word " go " meet with success, and having tasted it for a period, run into bad luck and disappointment for a further period. I have seen this happen so often and, unfortunately, have to admit that some were not able to take it, and threw in their hand; but the true enthusiast is made of sterner stuff, and carries on—what's more, he usually gets there, as he, like most sensible beings, knows that particularly in motor sport there is usually only one way, and that is the hard one, plus perhaps a little luck for good measure.

An injured Stanley Woods with 'Dippy' Harris at the 1934 Dublin 100 in the Phoenix Park.

This luck aspect, and also, I admit, a little bit of cheek, allied to the confidence of youth, decided my career for me. Just the lack of any one of these three ingredients would have forced me to tread a stonier path to the realms of international racing. This, briefly, is what happened:

At the age of 18, having competed with no success in a number of local events, viz., one road race, a couple of sand races, and a hill climb or two, in addition to a number of trials, and having watched the 1921 Isle of Man T.T. Races, I felt that an entry in the 1922 T.T. must be procured at all costs.

My finances were shaky, to say the least, but I had a vivid imagination; so I sat down and wrote to every motor cycle manufacturer I could think of and, to my surprise, received answers from all, the most encouraging being from the Cotton Motor Co. Their letter asked a number of leading questions as to my experience and ability. My reply must have been a masterpiece of suggestion and evasion, but it was backed up by letters of recommendation from a number of the Irish motor cycling " High-Ups ", and between us we convinced Mr. Cotton that I was the rider he had been looking for to complete his team for the Junior T.T.

I duly arrived on the Island in time for practising, and although nobody of 18 years of age looks exactly a greybeard, I, on the other hand, looked extremely youthful, perhaps two years younger; and when I was presented to Mr. Cotton, who was staking practically everything he had on the result of the race with his new machines, he just looked at me and said " Oh, good God ! " and strode out of the room.

Well, I didn't win the race, for a variety of reasons, the principal one being fire when refuelling at the end of the 2nd lap—this was followed by a broken valve push rod, complete failure of brakes on the 3rd lap, and a fall due to lack of brakes on the last lap. However, I managed to finish 5th, and in 1923, once again on a Cotton, had the satisfaction of winning the Junior T.T. at record speed.

I hope my little story serves to illustrate what I mean by an enthusiast, and I hope this book of Colley's will help all those who have followed the sport faithfully to recall the hard work and happiness they have experienced in its pursuit.

I think possibly one of the best features of the book is that it will appeal as readily to those who have no interest in motoring as to those who have. I have had fun reading it, and can only say " Thank you, Dudley".

STANLEY WOODS

FOREWORD

THIS NEW EDITION of Dudley Colley's book Wheel Patter, which is now edited and published by his son Tony, retains all the attractive qualities of the first edition. Tony has succeeded in bringing that golden era of the thirties right up to the present day.

'Wilf' Fitzsimmons at Enniskerry Hill Climb in his Bugatti

The book has now been enhanced by an important contribution from Tony, written in the same readable manner with which its author originally endowed it over fifty years ago.

When Dudley was kind enough to allow me to read his manuscript I was really impressed with it as, apart from the wholly natural and free flowing manner in which the story was told, it was an accurate chronicle of Irish Motor Sport at an era and time when the enthusiast, impecunious or otherwise had a pretty wide choice be, it of machines of two wheels or four.

There was plenty of choice, but the same could not be said of money, and consequently there was a great deal of ingenuity displayed by individuals in order to survive as regular competitors.

Up to this nobody in Ireland had produced a book about the trials and tribulations of the Sport and what a good story Dudley had to tell:

This was the era of the G.N. Cycle car and of course Frazer Nash, both chain driven and hugely popular with a large number of enthusiasts indeed - who came to be affectionately known in motor sport as the Chain Gang. Surely Dudley Colley typified the very essence of their attractive, if somewhat unconventional breed.

Wheel Patter was originally published in 1951 by the Talbot Press in Dublin for whom I worked, and I had the pleasure of successfully recommending the acceptance of Dudley's manuscript, and feel this new edition will be welcomed by all enthusiasts, in particular the Chain Gang – old and not so old.

WILFORD FITZSIMMONS

CONTENTS

WHEEL PATTER

CHAPTER I.
Heredity or Environment?

I AM not an authority on heredity, but it is an undeniable fact that my father was an ardent 'automobilist' in his day. Perhaps this is why my life has been dominated by motor vehicles-not ordinary, sensible motor cars, but queer contrivances that had to be noisier, smellier, and dirtier than anyone else's.

The author's father in the Argyll which he drove to Heidelberg in 1907

Father started motoring in 1903, and he had toured the length and breadth of Ireland, and a great deal of the Continent before the death of King Edward. He did not go in for competitive motoring to any extent, but I have found one contemporary account of a hill climb in the beautiful

Glendhu Valley, in which he won his class with a 10 h.p. Argyll in 1905. In those days, of course, the idea of a hill climb was to find out which car could climb the chosen hill under its own power, and not as to-day when it is the fastest possible ascent that counts.

There is no evidence that my father did much mechanical work, other than the usual running repairs, but he was a trained engineer, having passed through the Engineering School of Trinity College. Among his collection of books l have found many finely drawn designs for steam engines, such as were popular in Victorian mechanical text books.

My grandfather also was a keen motorist and his favourite car was an enormous Minerva, painted a brilliant yellow and fitted with a wickerwork umbrella holder and picnic basket. He drove it about the country at most unsuitable speeds and in clouds of dust, frightening horses and murdering chickens, and it became known far and wide as the 'Yellow Peril'. I well remember the polished brass fittings and the steady drip of the row of oil feeds on the dash-board.

I was thus born into an atmosphere of motoring. The walls of this old country house, instead of being adorned with the usual hunting scenes and trophies of the chase, have rows of early photographs of high, stilted cars, bowler-hatted and bewhiskered drivers, and ladies of the family in enormous dust veils. The lumber lofts still hold ancient steel-studded leather-bound tyres. Even the tractor driver on the farm still refers to a spare wheel as a 'Stepney'.

Thinking back to childhood days, I have no recollection of being particularly interested in mechanical things, but the older locals assure me that I spent most of my time in the coach house, watching the 'chauffeur' at work. This gentleman was just the handyman about the place, but of course no one could have a motor without a chauffeur. Then I believe that at school I earned the reputation of being something of the 'mad inventor' type. Most of the precious playtime was spent in designing peculiar and impractical steam cars.

CHAPTER II.
First Symptoms.

IT was not till I reached the age of fifteen or sixteen that I began to think about the average boy's dream to own a motor-cycle.

Once the idea of a motor-cycle had taken hold, it could not be shaken off. The chauffeur was pestered to use his influence with the motor trade, and every lorry driver that visited the farm was forced to promise faithfully that he would search the country.

Finally, it was one of these lorry men who brought me the good news. He had located a machine which he considered was just what I wanted, and what was more, the price was only £4.

To raise a sum of money such as £4 is to the average schoolboy an almost insurmountable problem. There are, of course, the lucky few who are gifted with a pleading expression which is irresistible to indulgent parents. There are some well-endowed with generous and wealthy uncles and godparents, whose annual contributions far exceed the normal requirements in toys and sweets. There are also the thrifty-minded who actually manage to save from their weekly pocket-money.

I cannot say that I could be classed with any of these types, although my parents were by no means stinting in their gifts, both in and out of season; but there were six of us in the family, so that the even distribution of any presents, however small, amounted to quite a large disbursement. And so, when my heart became set on possessing a motor-cycle, there is no doubt that my finances were at a very low ebb. I had, however, one card to play and now I considered was the time to use it.

It seems that many years before the time of which I write a lamb had been born on the farm, and had been left motherless. I was given the job of bottle-feeding the orphan, and in the course of time the lamb, having survived my administrations, became a sheep and joined the main flock. It was, however, always regarded as my particular lamb, and when it was eventually sold, I laid claim to its price, which happened to be four pounds. I was told that this money would be kept in trust until I was older, and when there might be something that I really wanted.

Now, I considered, was the time when no better use could be made of this so far frozen asset. I approached my father diffidently and haltingly made my plea. It worked, and I was somewhat doubtfully handed out four beautiful pound notes. Thinking it over, I have an idea that this very stratagem had been used before, and that my now rusting push bicycle had been procured by drawing on the same 'lamb money', but this was no time to think of such things – I had the price of my motor-cycle, and that was all that mattered.

In due course the money changed hands, the machine arrived on a lorry, and was reverently unloaded in the yard. I cannot describe the overwhelming feeling of excitement and anticipation at that moment. In future years, when many more potent and desirable vehicles came into my possession, I had at least some idea of what their performance would be. Now I was entering into unknown realms of speed and power.

Note that there was no careful perusal of manufacturers' catalogues; no detailed inspection in garage showrooms; no engineer's report, or trial run. I wanted a motor-cycle, and as far as I knew it was a motor-cycle at which I was now gazing in rapt admiration. I must admit that it did not look very like the shiny, red racers that appeared in the illustrations in my boys' adventure books; but it had an engine and a petrol tank, and anyway, who was I to judge? At that time I didn't know a Norton from a Francis Barnett, nor a four-stroke from a two-stroke.

The lorryman, having completed the deal, left me to my own devices, and I have a strong suspicion that he knew even less about it than I did. I think he just did not want to be there to witness the first run. I therefore applied myself to the task of finding out what all the taps and levers did, mostly by following all the Bowden cables from lever to source, and actuating them to see what happened. I actually had a smattering of book-knowledge on the subject, as I had found in the shelves of my father's study a handbook on The Light Motor-Bicycle. It was dated 1903, and according to its pages, all motor-cycles had pedals, a long belt from engine to back wheel, and a supply of batteries that somehow produced a spark. My machine seemed altogether different. It was, in fact, an Ivy two-stroke of about 200 c.c. It had a two-speed gearbox and belt drive, a 'spoon' brake on the belt pulley, and a magneto driven by an exposed chain. I think it was manufactured in 1920. In all the years I have only seen one other machine of this make.

1920 Ivy two-stroke

I cannot now remember how long it was before I actually got it to run, but I remember days and days of pushing and kicking and plug-cleaning and jet-clearing. I think I must have pushed it quite as far as it ran under its own power in those first weeks. I was lucky in living on a farm, as I had a fair stretch of lanes and avenues on which to do my testing, and I had not to worry about such things as road tax and driving licence.

There followed many months of thinking and dreaming motor-cycling - but very little actual motor-cycling. Holidays were mostly spent in impatiently waiting for some part or other to be repaired in Dublin workshops; term time was whiled away in harrying the unfortunate manufacturers with endless correspondence, asking for advice and instructions and lists of spare parts and improvements. Looking back, one must admire the stoic patience of these good people who, although they must have known from my writing that I was only a schoolboy, would answer fully and helpfully any query I sent them; they certainly got very little money out of me.

At about this time, the summer of 1927, I managed to gain a little more experience of motor-cycling, in a highly illegal way. I had a school friend who was bitten with the same disease, and he had managed to smuggle a machine into an old shed near the school in England where we were both supposed to be receiving our education. This was an ancient Triumph, its main features being a large four-stroke engine and an enormous three-speed hub gear in the back wheel, exactly like the normal push-bike hub gear but about six times as big. We spent many happy hours taking this machine to bits and reassembling it when we should have been playing cricket, and we eventually got it into a condition in which it would run. It was, of course, strictly against the rules to have a motor-cycle at school, but the desire to take it out and test it was unconquerable. Accordingly, a whispered plot was hatched, and at five o'clock one summer morning we both slid down the fire-escapes of our respective dormitories and crept to our shed. The machine was wheeled out and pushed quietly to a straight stretch of road some distance from the village. It started easily, and a blissful half-hour was spent tearing up and down the road. It was then pushed back to its shed and we were back in bed, glowing with fresh air and satisfaction, long before the school was astir.

Of course, once having tasted this joy (and having got away with it), it had to be repeated. It was now imperative to find out what speed the machine would attain, so there was further plotting and scheming. We decided that we must have a third person to help with our timing arrangements, so a likely enthusiast was co-opted from the motor-minded element in the Lower Fourth. Two somewhat unreliable stop-watches were purloined from the science laboratory, and an evening was spent pacing and measuring a half-mile strip on our chosen piece of country road. The next morning at daybreak the three conspirators crept out as before, the machine was wheeled out and the time-keepers set their watches and took up position. Several runs in both directions were made in the approved manner, the times being carefully noted on prepared time-sheets, to be translated into terms of miles-per-hour later, probably during a Latin class. However, either our capacity for sustained effort in mathematical calculations was insufficient or our watches were more uncertain than we had imagined. The final result showed a gradual crescendo of speed, ranging from about 30 m.p.h. for the first run to something over 200 m.p.h. for the last, which even in our most optimistic moments we knew must have been rather unlikely.

I do not know how many more of these early morning adventures might have taken place, but unfortunately, my friend's parents, who were somewhat less indulgent than mine, became alarmed at the standard of his school reports, and shortly afterwards he and his motor-cycle disappeared from among us. I have never heard of him since.

My experience with the Triumph had added a good deal of useful material to my knowledge of motor-cycling, and when I got home I was able to get my own machine to run well enough to justify taxing it for use on the public highway and providing myself with a driving licence. There was no compulsory insurance in those days. I made many trips, some of them as far as 20 miles from home. I began to take an interest in racing, as a spectator of course, and went to see the famous 'Leinster Hundred' which took place at Skerries at that time, and I remember being vastly impressed by the performance of the Coventry Eagle two-strokes, which were of much smaller capacity than my own machine, but seemed to get along at prodigious speeds. I also followed in the wake of reliability trials, and spent many days trying to get through some of the easier sections near my home. One of my great ambitions was to climb a certain hill known as Killinarden, without running alongside. It is one of the steepest roads in the country. and brings most modern cars down to their lowest gear. Needless to say, I never succeeded and could often be seen lying exhausted beside my overheated bicycle, having run beside it almost to the top.

Whatever the faults of this beloved machine, possession of it taught me more about what could go wrong with a motorcycle in a shorter time than I could have learnt in any other way. By leaving me stranded far from home it taught me self-reliance and how to improvise repairs in the face of difficulties. One instance of this stands out in my memory: I was nearing the foot of Killinarden for one of my assaults on the hill, when the belt broke at the fastener. I had no proper tools with me and I found I was helpless without a vice in which to hold the fastener while I refitted it. Glancing round in despair, I found I was sitting on the line of the old Blessington steam tramway, and right beside me was the lever operating the points which let the trams pass one another on the single line. Here right at my hand was a perfect vice. I placed the fastener between the rails, moved the lever just enough to grip it, inserted the various screws and hooks, and the job was done. On another occasion I actually mended a puncture with some tar scraped from the road and a piece of American cloth torn from the cover of a pocket-book. Many a fence in the district gave pieces of wire to hold on the more important accessories when they were inclined to fall off.

This machine also taught me what it is to be frightened on a motor-cycle; not that its own speed capabilities when under its own power would alarm an octogenarian, but on this occasion it was on the end of a tow rope. I had travelled about ten miles from home, when the primary chain broke, and in lashing round had removed the whole contact-breaker from the magneto. I had not been contemplating the wreckage for long when a motor-cyclist passed, and with the usual camaraderie of these people (I still didn't regard myself as a motor-cyclist) he stopped and offered me a tow home. I gladly accepted the offer and a suitable piece of rope was found, which I in my ignorance tied to the forks of my machine. I was soon to find out that my Good Samaritan friend was the rider of an extremely powerful and inflexible racing machine, with a bottom gear which didn't allow it to progress at less than about 40 miles an hour. We proceeded in a series of rushes, and every time the rope slackened it caught under the front mudguard and lifted the front wheel high in the air. My companion proceeded in this way, all the way to my gate, quite unaware of my terrified yells for mercy. When we stopped my knees just gave away under me, and I vowed that I would never be towed again without a 'slippery hitch' on the tow rope.

The end of this, my first machine, was somewhat ignominious; I was greatly over-revving it in low gear while on a trip in the Dublin mountains. This was too much for the longsuffering crankshaft which parted just behind the flywheel boss. The flywheel dropped on the road, paused for a second spinning wildly, and then dashed off down the road, jumped over the low bank, and bounded off across the heather like a pursued antelope. I never saw it again. I still come across bits of the old Ivy when rooting through a big box in my workshop labelled 'SCRAP'.

CHAPTER III.
Logical Development - Two Wheels to Four

THE end of my first motor-cycle coincided, roughly speaking, with the end of my schooldays; my parents had come to the conclusion that I was of a mechanical turn of mind, and it was decided that, with my approval, I should enter Trinity College, Dublin, and study for an engineering degree. The idea was that I should live at home and go in daily to attend lectures, and it was therefore essential (so I insisted) to have a car. At this time I had had my fill of motor-cycling, though later on I found the urge to return to two wheels irresistible.

The type of car I wanted was something small and sporting in appearance, and of course, open to the elements. I proceeded to do the rounds of the Dublin garages and scrap yards which had become familiar to me in the past couple of years. There were many vehicles for sale, but there seemed to be few of the kind I required. At one place I saw a machine that had me sorely tempted; it was a G.N., painted fire-engine red, low and rakish, and two motor-cycle type cylinders sticking out through the bonnet. It was, however, in a somewhat dilapidated condition and the price demanded was £40, which even to my inexperienced eye seemed very much on the high side. I have never ceased to regret failing to gain possession of this machine, and it was not till some three or four years later that I joined the ranks of the 'Chain Gang', that proud if eccentric band of G.N. and Frazer Nash owners.

The car I eventually acquired was a Standard Nine two seater with dickey, built in about 1923. Now the Standard Motor Company have built many first-class cars before and since, but either they slipped up badly with this particular model, or it had received much brutal treatment before it came into my possession. Whatever the cause, the less said about this car the better; my parents were staggered at the bills for repairs, and forthwith decided that the only solution was a New Car. This time it was not necessary to go round the garages; the car was chosen by the simple expedient of finding the cheapest new car on the market. Needless to say, this was the famous Austin Seven open tourer of the year1930

My feelings on becoming the proud owner of this wonderful little car were curiously mixed; it was not really the kind of machine I wanted; something racier, that I could take to pieces and 'improve' was more in my line. It was so shiny and new and perfect that I wouldn't dare to put a spanner to it. At the same time I had to admit how lucky I was to own a brand new car at the age of nineteen. Anyway, whatever my inner thoughts, I was outwardly delighted with it, and I treated it with all the love and care that such a car deserved. I ran it in carefully, if impatiently, had it serviced regularly, polished and cleaned it like a Rolls Royce. When it was run in, I found that it was remarkably lively, and I am afraid that I began to exploit its speed capabilities to the full, and not always in the most favourable circumstances.

All was well, if perhaps a little humdrum, for the first couple of months or so, and then came my first major accident. I happened to be late one morning and was hurrying in to College for a nine o'clock lecture. The road was wet and greasy, and the speed was far in excess of what the most liberally minded could call safe. A bus crossed my path on its lawful business; I applied the brakes, turned backwards, and hit the bus squarely amidships. The chassis of the Austin did its best to pass under the bus, but the body was left on the road with me still in it, completely unhurt but suitably cowed. Later, there were the usual police court proceedings, and I well remember the impassioned plea which the solicitor of one of the motoring organisations put up on my behalf. But the justice had heard it all before, and I was suitably fined and went on my way, a wiser and poorer student.

It took six weeks and a good deal of my insurance company's funds to piece my little car together again, but in due course it was handed back to me looking none the worse for its first, repeat, its first crash.

After this episode, I drove with decorum at any rate for a while; but the sobering effect of a bad smash soon began to wear off, and if anything, I drove harder than ever. There seemed to be only two suitable positions for the throttle pedal - fully up, and fully down; harsh treatment for a little runabout that was originally designed to take old ladies on shopping expeditions at 25 miles per hour.

1930 Austin 7 "Chummy" Open tourer

I had very little mechanical trouble, but for one curious weakness, or perhaps it was not so curious when one considers the circumstances. One day, when I was exploring the Dublin hills, I was left stranded by the breaking of a half-shaft. The car was brought to Messrs. Crawford's, the highly respectable agents from whom it had been purchased, and it was duly fitted with a new shaft, I think under the maker's guarantee. It was not long, however, before it was back again with the other shaft broken, also in the Dublin hills. Again it was brought to Mr. Fox, the patient foreman, and again another shaft was fitted. In the next few months two more half-shafts broke, to the complete bewilderment of Messrs. Crawford's garage staff. The car was carefully checked over, but no cause could be found for this weakness. Half-shafts had been known to break, but never four on the same car in as many months. Mr. Fox asked me earnestly if I could give any clue as to the cause of the trouble.

' Well," I suggested, "I don't know if this could have anything to do with it, but I often notice when going round a corner fast that the inside rear wheel lifts off the road and spins violently. Perhaps the shaft breaks when the wheel hits the road again."

I got out of the garage without receiving any physical violence, but it was many months before I dared show my face there again.

I began to develop a deep affection for this heroic little car, and in its short life it provided me with a wealth of motoring experience, both amusing and otherwise, comic and serious. It was also the machine in which I first took part in competition.

This first competition was a gymkhana for motor cars, held in the grounds of a country house near Castleknock, and run more or less on the lines of the pony events usually held on these occasions. There were potato races and cream bun-eating competitions and manoeuvring tests rather like the tests in modern reliability trials. Owing to the extreme handiness of the Austin Seven, and the abandon with which I drove it, I won most of the events (except, needless to say, the 'slow race'), but I must admit that most of my rivals were ladies of the district, driving ponderous family saloons.

Even this very unimportant event gave me a taste and thirst for motor sport which I have never been able to shake off, and it was not long before I had entered for a sand race to be held on the beach at Portmarnock.

CHAPTER IV.
The Urge to Compete

OF all forms of motor sport, sand racing is probably the hardest on the machine. The mixture of fine sand and sea water has a disastrous effect on wheel bearings and seems to find its way into every corner of the vehicle, and the salt water has a peculiar chemical effect on all aluminium and copper parts. Consequently, only the madder enthusiasts are to be found among those who take part.

The races held in 1932 by the Trinity College club—which has the rather ponderous title, The Dublin University Motor-Cycle and Light Car Club—proved no exception as far as entries were concerned. There were motor-cycles in plenty but only half-a-dozen cars, entered by owners who didn't know or didn't care what would happen. I think I would be classed with both categories—I didn't know the ill-effects of sand in the works, and even if I knew, it wasn't going to stop me from having a go.

Sand racing in itself is great fun, and particularly suited my somewhat ham-fisted style of driving. There is nothing for miles around to run into, and one can go into the corners flat out, the only danger being the possibility of turning over. To counteract this tendency I had as passenger some 14 stone of ardent motor-cyclist, one Harry Carson, who was a fellow-student and also the son of the rector of my home parish. Harry had a penchant for side-car racing, and during these events as my passenger he performed all the acrobatic feats that these people enact as a matter of course in what is perhaps the most spectacular form of motor-cycle racing. He seemed to hold on by his toes and lean inwards on the corners till his head (on which he took the precaution of wearing a crash helmet) almost touched the ground. In actual fact, he was rather lucky not to receive a grave injury, because his necktie came adrift and became entangled in the spokes of a rear wheel as he was hanging upside down over the side. Luckily the tie ripped apart, so Harry was not 'drawn into the works'.

As to the races, I need hardly add that we did not figure in the results; a 'chummy' Austin Seven is hardly the right machine for this form of competition. Nevertheless, I thoroughly enjoyed myself, and my appetite was whetted for any kind of motor sport. Later on, the Austin was to be entered in many reliability trials, but it was never used for speed events again as it was obviously quite unsuitable.

Shortly after the Portmarnock event I had an opportunity to do some touring, and one trip in England is worthy of being recorded because of certain incidents.

A college friend, Desmond FitzGerald Finch, invited me to spend a few days with his people who lived near the South coast of England. We thought it would be a good idea to pool our resources and to take the Austin across, and also to make a tour of it and visit our old schools. In due course one of the motoring organisations produced the necessary triptyque and supplied us with itineraries; international driving licences were obtained and the car, loaded with luggage, was shipped to Holyhead.

So far all went well. The next step was to clear the customs, and at this point we were dumbfounded on being told that a deposit of one-third the value of the car was required. We asked why this should be so, and the reason was given that in the last couple of days it had been discovered that the Austin Sevens of that year were fitted with horns of foreign manufacture. We protested that we had been told nothing about this in Dublin and were obviously not in a position to put down the £30 demanded. The customs officers, however, were adamant, and there was nothing for it but to wire home explanations and to ask that a money order for the amount should he sent on as soon as possible. Nothing had arrived by nightfall, so we had to find digs in the not too exciting town of Holyhead, and kick our heels and curse our luck. The money order arrived next morning from benevolent parents, and we started on our way at midday, having wasted a day and a half of our precious time.

After an uneventful journey we reached our first objective, which was my old school near Derby. This was rather a depressing experience as, of course, the boys were away for the holidays and the place had a 'deserted village' air. All attempts to find anyone that I had known during my school days failed, so we decided to move on, with spirits rather low; but it was cheering to drive over the stretch of road where once I had ridden a motor-cycle surreptitiously by dawn's early light, now in a perfectly respectable and legal motor car.

Having shaken the dust of Repton from our wheels, we set off in a, roughly, southerly direction, without having any very clear idea of where we were going. It was getting somewhat late and we were beginning to think of somewhere to spend the night, when the magic word 'OXFORD' on a signpost reminded me that I had a cousin in the area who would be sure to put us up. This cousin, Elizabeth Bowen, was at that time well on the road to success in the literary field and was later to become a very famous authoress; she was also a very good friend and I knew that she would be very pleased to put her house at our disposal. Consequently, when we eventually located the house after travelling many miles and making many enquiries, we were not over-dismayed to find it in darkness and deserted. I told myself that if we could find our way in, we could make ourselves comfortable and await her return, and I was sure she would be surprised and delighted to see us. Such is the precocity of youth.

It did not take us long to cross the garden wall, find the usual window which had been left unlatched—it is extraordinary how there is always one window forgotten in every house—let ourselves in, turned on lights and radio, and generally made ourselves welcome.

I think we were in the middle of our second cup of tea when there was a loud knocking at the door and the stentorian voice of doom: "Open, in the name of the law." Outside was the local constable, who regarded us with the greatest suspicion (remember, we were near the University town of Oxford) and demanded who we were and what we were doing in a house which, according to him, was owned by a lady who had gone away for a few days and had put her house under police protection in her absence. We haltingly tried to explain ourselves and I must say our story sounded very unlikely when told under the gaze of a very doubting constable. Even at the best of times, and in the most innocent circumstances, I become tongue-tied when confronted by the arm of the law.

Our policeman was also rather at a loss as to what he should do; our Irish papers and car full of luggage added weight to our story, but people just didn't do that sort of thing in law-abiding England. He decided he must consult his sergeant, and having warned us to stay where we were, he took his departure. We decided that we had caused enough trouble for one night, and now was the chance to make ourselves scarce. We hastily tidied the house, scribbled note for Elizabeth, locked up, tumbled into the car, and were away with one idea, to put as many miles as possible between us and Oxford in the shortest possible time. For the second time on our trip we had rather sheepishly set off again with no definite objective.

By this time it was well after midnight, and we raced through the darkness expecting, as we passed through each sleeping village and as we rounded each bend, to find the full force of the police of England out to stop us and bring us to justice. This put all other thought out of our heads, and we were taken completely by surprise when the little car faltered and came to a halt with a very empty petrol tank. Even an Austin Seven won't run for ever on a tankful, and the necessity for filling up had missed our attention.

There was nothing for it but to push the car in the direction it was pointing and hope for the best. We had no idea where we were or what the best we hoped for would turn out to be. At this point the guardian angel appointed to look after motorists decided it was time to render aid; after about two miles of steady pushing, a large roadside filling station came into sight. It seemed completely deserted, but as we looked around, and even toyed with the idea of breaking the lock on one of the pumps, we saw a sight that I had never seen before or since. One of the pumps had a large notice stating that if we put a shilling in the slot we would be served with the equivalent value of the best motor spirit. Luckily we had the necessary shilling, and soon we were on our way with sufficient petrol for another 25 or 30 miles, which proved quite enough to take us to an all-night garage where we filled up to the top and were on our way, still southwards but otherwise with no idea of our goal.

Shortly afterwards, the mental and physical strains we had undergone began to tell on us, and I found myself overcome with that bane of night-driving—unconquerable sleepiness. Try as I would, I could not keep my eyes open, and after I had twice woken to find myself motoring on the footpath, I decided it was essential to stop and take a nap. We pulled into the side and settled ourselves for a short sleep in the car. Now I am nearly six feet, and my friend Desmond was six foot four, so sleeping in an Austin Seven filled with luggage meant sleeping in a bolt-upright position with the chin resting on the chest, the hands folded on the stomach. After about five minutes of trying to woo slumber in this position, the humour of the situation suddenly struck both of us simultaneously. The result was a good laugh which effectively shook all thoughts of sleep, and we set off again.

Now, as the light of dawn began to spread around us, glimpses of occasional signposts showed us that we were quite within striking distance of my friend's home, and we decided to press on. With a definite objective ahead, driving seemed much easier and we reached Desmond's home in time to have a bath and a shave before a large breakfast, having driven some 330 miles since the previous midday. This does not seem a great feat in the light of later experience, but at the time we were very pleased with ourselves. We heard nothing more of the Oxford affair, but my cousin later told me that it had caused quite a sensation at the Oxford County police headquarters.

During my stay at the FitzGerald Finch home I was to add a little to my motoring experience by driving some miles in one of those amazing and unconventional cars—the Trojan. This car had a two-stroke engine under the seats, chain drive, and narrow solid tyres. It was said that its track coincided with that of the normal tramcar, and if the driver was unlucky enough to slip into the rail grooves it was necessary to go to the tram terminus in order to get out of them again. I believe these cars gave good and reliable service to those who were not too fussy about creature comforts and I have seen accounts of one performing well in recent reliability trials.

There is little to add, from the motoring point of view, to this account of our tour in England, but there was one little bit of diversion which may amuse readers who are not too sceptical. We were near the end of the trip, and travelling well along the coast road in North Wales, headed for Holyhead, and with not too much time to spare to catch the boat for Dublin. Now the map-reading capabilities of myself and my crew were at a very low level, and by this time we had long since ceased to look at maps at all; they always seemed to lead us astray. To add to this, in my case at any rate, I seem to have been born without any 'bump of locality' or sense of direction; these failings have been a constant handicap to me, particularly in trials and mountain runs.

In this case, however, we knew we were on the north coast of Wales and travelling westward; logically, we thought, if we keep going sooner or later we were bound to come to Anglesea, and thence to Holyhead. After some time, we came to a seaside town, Llandudno I think it was, but I have not verified this as I don't want to spoil my story for the sake of a little geographical accuracy.

We left this town by a rugged coast road, and after a couple of miles we came to another town. Neither of us was particularly observant, but both were struck by the resemblance to the town we had just left. Desmond said: "Did you notice rather a peculiar thing? All the picture houses in this town are showing the same films as in the town we have just left." I also had rather an uneasy feeling that something was wrong, but we carried on through the town and again left it by a rugged coast road. We had not gone very far before we both got the I-have-been-here-before feeling so strongly that it couldn't be dismissed. But we had never left the coast, so how could we be travelling the same ground twice? We rooted out the map and examined it minutely, and there before us was the solution; it appeared that there was a sort of peninsula, almost an island joined to the town, which had a rocky scenic road right round it and so designed to bring the sightseer back to his starting point. Anyway, that's my story and I'm sticking to it.

We finally caught the boat with a few minutes to spare, and that was the end of our tour in England.

CHAPTER V.
Clash of Interests

WHILE I was in College and supposed to be studying engineering I decided that I must take part in College sport, and as I had always had a taste for the water, I joined the Dublin University Boat Club. Rowing is a fine sport which teaches self-denial and endurance and exercises every muscle in the body. When after a suitable period as a tyro I was made a member of a 'maiden' crew, rowing introduced me to the scenic beauty and quiet waters of most of the rivers and harbours of Ireland.

It was in connection with rowing, and the seasonal round of the provincial regattas that my little Austin became invaluable, not only to myself but to the favoured members of the crew who could be squeezed in. Indeed this squeezing in was sometimes taken to extremes and I remember on one occasion, when we were competing at a regatta in Coleraine and having hotel accommodation in Portrush, seven hefty oarsmen managed to get on board and were carried both ways without mishap.

Limerick Regatta was an event which received the regular Support of the Trinity Club, and on one occasion four members of the maiden crew, including myself, went down in the Austin. After the races there was the usual gala dance, which went on into the early hours of the morning, and as funds for hotel bills were short, we decided to return to Dublin with the idea of getting home in time for breakfast. Such is the endurance of Man in his early twenties.

I do not remember at what time we left the southern city, but the little car buzzed its way homewards without a hint of protest. As we came on to the sweeping, gorse-covered downs of the famous Curragh in County

Kildare the sun was rising to herald a beautiful day. The view was one which has always stuck in my memory, and it was to be permanently imprinted there by an incident which happened in the next few moments.

We decided we must stop by the roadside to enjoy to the full this lovely, sparkling dawn, and also to stretch our very cramped limbs. As we climbed from the car the air was suddenly filled with equine snortings and the sound of wildly galloping hooves; the plains of the Curragh seemed to be full of flying, bucking horses and somersaulting stable lads. As we stopped we had quite failed to notice the approach of a string of two-year-olds out for their early morning exercise from the racing stables of the Curragh, and the sight of four wild-looking young men in fiercely striped rowing blazers emerging from the tiny car had been too much for these excitable thoroughbreds, who promptly got rid of their riders and disappeared over the horizon in the shortest possible time. We decided that this might not be the healthiest spot from which to admire the view, and hastily tumbled into the Austin and made off rapidly in the rough direction of Dublin.

....

Anyone who wishes to indulge in more than one form of sport will sooner or later be troubled by a clash of interests; I was no exception.

In my case, the sport of rowing involved 'team spirit" while motoring, in the form in which I hoped to take part, was largely an individual affair. The result was that rowing usually took precedence, as of course crews could not be let down by the absence of even a single member. I need hardly add that this caused much mental stress and heartburning.

It happened that in June, 1931, my crew was down to row a match in Enniskillen in Northern Ireland, which is about 120 miles from my home. Imagine my horror when I discovered that the date coincided with the Phoenix Park Grand Prix—the last of the famous series run by the R.I.A.C. I had been looking forward to this event as only a motor-mad enthusiast of 19 can; I had attended all the early morning practices and could see that it would be a first-class race.

The rowing event was to take place in the morning, so I reckoned that if I could get away early and put in some fast motoring, I could get back to Dublin in time to see at least some of the Grand Prix. But I had left out of my calculations the ceremonious luncheon to which we were to be invited by our vanquished opponents, and I knew that it would be unpolitic, not to say impolite, to slip away before this function.

I think I have never enjoyed a luncheon less, and the post-prandial speeches were just agony, and at the earliest opportunity I mumbled my excuses and slipped away. There followed one of the most hair-raising drives my little Austin had ever been asked to endure, as I rushed for Dublin in the faint hope of seeing the final stages of the battle which I could almost hear being fought out in the Phoenix Park. Now Enniskillen is in Northern Ireland, which meant that there would be tedious delays at the Customs posts, but as I approached the control hut, the place seemed deserted; I suppose the officers were at their lunch or otherwise occupied. I decided to damn the consequences, and drove through and onwards with even increased speed as I imagined squads of border police on my tail. Nothing happened, however, and in due course I neared the Park in something over three hours for the trip. But as I approached the gates I was faced by a solid stream of race-gorged spectators, pouring out in their thousands, having witnessed what was to be the last big race in

Southern Ireland for many years. I could not fight my way in against the stream, in the hope of browsing round the rapidly emptying pits, to pick up stray fragments of after-race gossip, or the last fragrant whiffs of hot racing oil.

Later on, this clash of divided interests was to frustrate me again, and I was to be informed through the medium of a telegram that a car of my own construction had won its class in a hill-climb in the hands of a friend—while I was bursting my blood-vessels rowing over the boat race course at Putney, London.

CHAPTER VI.

"All Play and No Work...."

THE object of those years of my education which I spent under the august and endearing patronage of that ancient institution, Trinity College, Dublin, was to teach me engineering and so to send me out into the world armed with that passport to the honoured profession, the Engineering Degree. I am not very clear what I intended to do if and when I got it, and I was living very much in the present—the future seemed so very far away.

For my part, I was very disappointed to find that the course was largely a civil engineering one, and I am afraid I lapsed into bored slumber or back-row poker games when the subject to be absorbed was the building of roads, bridges, or even roof-trusses. It was only when we moved to the power-house to conduct brake tests on somewhat antiquated gas-engines that I began to sit up and take notice; but even then I found myself more concerned with how to get more revs out of the old engine, than to appreciate the finer points of how the actual test was carried out.

One of the main features of the Middle Year of the course was an operation known as 'Road Improvement in the Phoenix Park'. The piece of road chosen was a beautiful stretch of several hairpin bends and sweeping curves on the south side of the Park, and the object was to survey this terrain with a view to replacing the twisting road with a fine, straight, modern carriageway.

Now there was a small car-owning motor-sport-minded section of our class who considered that this road was perfectly all right the way it was. It was a perfect joy to drive on, and the hairpin bends produced exciting slides and squealing tyres; it was a road on which neat gear-changing was a necessity. This section of the class could be distinguished from the rest by a glance in the drawing office; the title on the drawing board of any of these enthusiasts was sure to read 'Road ALTERATION in the Phoenix Park' instead of the official nomenclature.

Not only was our road a pleasant test of skill in itself, but it could also be linked up by other Park roads to form a grand little racing circuit. No sooner was this fact discovered and tested, than it became highly desirable to both organise and take part in a race there. So while the more earnest students were gazing in their theodolites, or trudging along with their chains and their surveyor's staffs and generally behaving like budding civil engineers, the more irresponsible element was lining up for the start of the Middle Year Grand Prix.

This particular stretch of road had been used as a surveying exercise for the past twenty years; the same kindly professor had been in charge of the operation, and he had used the same cab, the same jarvey, and probably the same horse, to carry him from College to the scene of operations, all through the years. It was, therefore, rather the hand of fate than ordinary bad luck which brought our professor and his cab on to the course from the opposite end, just as we were going nicely on the second lap.

I suppose the old horse had never moved quicker as he swerved the cab up on to the steep bank beside the road. As we flashed by we saw the roof of the yoke, which was piled high with theodolites, levels, staffs, and all the impedimenta of the surveyor, shower its load over the road. We also caught a glimpse of the scandalised face of our chief.

We, the culprits, disappeared round a bend, hid our cars in neighbouring bushes, and by the time the professor had collected his scattered thoughts and instruments, we were in various parts of the area, gazing earnestly through levels and making meaningless notes in dirty little notebooks.

A great deal was said, but nothing drastic ever happened as a result of this episode.

....

Engineering students, as a breed, have a peculiar sense of humour which is inclined to appear on the surface in the form of practical jokes. This may be a direct reaction to the daily absorption of somewhat dry but useful instruction, or it may be that the mental processes are synonymous.

Whether it shows itself in the simple whim of placing a cigarette butt between the lips of the venerable statues of past Provosts, or the concocting of miniature atom bombs in the chemistry laboratories and placing them in the drawing office stove—the mentality is the same.

For some reason, a very small car is the ideal butt for the practical joker, and the presence of my Baby Austin outside the Engineering School was a providential gift to these subnormals. Whenever I came to fetch it, I could never be sure from day to day where or in what condition I would find it. These pranks usually were simple things, such as hiding it in the bushes, or crossing the spark-plug wires, or corking up the exhaust pipe; sometimes they went to greater lengths. On one occasion I suffered the indignity of being stopped by the porters from driving out through the Front Gate with the groundsman's rubber-tyred trolley attached behind; on another day my car was found parked at the top of the marble staircase in the Engineering School. Heaven knows what effort and how many students were involved in this task. Many years later I got the credit for having driven it up the stairs, but it was a considerable feat even to drive it down.

I remember once, seeking to get into the good graces of the geology professor, shortly before exam-time,

I offered to drive him to the quarry-site outside Dublin, where we were to examine the strata formation. All went well for a time' and then a peculiarly unpleasant fishy odour began to permeate the atmosphere in the car. I dared not remark on it, just in case it might be emanating from the professor. He, on his part, was too much a gentleman to mention it, in case it came from his driver. The journey continued in somewhat embarrassed silence, with the smell getting steadily more pronounced. When we finally arrived I got rid of my professor and opened the bonnet in search of the cause. There, bound tightly to the exhaust pipe, was a Very Old Kipper.

....

Although the preceding paragraphs may give the impression that I was always at the receiving end of the practical jokes, this was not strictly the case; in fact I could give quite as good as I got, but I cannot say that I derived much pleasure from it. I am, by nature, somewhat sensitive and the sight of even the most temporary discomfiture of my victim would work on my sympathies. The feeling was not strong enough, at one time, to prevent me from jacking up the rear wheel of a car, the property of a rather unmechanically minded professor of the classics, and to watch from the Engineering School windows his perplexed expression as he tried to drive off in all his academic dignity.

Although this sensitivity, or weakness of mind, or whatever the psycho-analysts may call it, curbed my enterprise in the field of practical jokes, it was also the direct cause of involving me in another form of foolish escapade. I never could resist or refuse, if dared to do anything which might demonstrate the ability of my Austin to do things that could not be done by other motor cars.

One day a group of students was gathered in Botany Bay, which at that time was the centre of motoring in College, being the official 'car park'. We were discussing driving judgement, and I was foolish enough to boast that I could judge the width of my car to within two inches. I was promptly challenged to prove this, and after a little argument a suitable test was devised.

I was to go out into the Front Square, and from the middle I was to look at the Campanile. If I thought my car would fit through the arch at the base, I was to drive through, at not less than 20 miles per hour.

Now, for the benefit of those of my readers who do not know Trinity College, I must explain that the Campanile is an imposing, if not beautiful structure—the centre piece of the Front Square and, in fact, more or less the centre of the whole College. It is a form of arch, surmounted by a dome, containing, I believe, a bell. The arch is ornamental rather than functional, and not intended for traffic. To make sure that it is not used for such, there is now a large iron post in the middle.

Having made my boast, and having been dared to test it, there was no turning back. I drove slowly out into the square and faced the arch, hoping against hope that it would be obviously too narrow to attempt; but unfortunately it looked as if it could just be done. I gritted my teeth and drove straight at it, with the speedometer needle as near to 20 as I could get it....

Yes, I would like this story to go down in print as a tribute to my prowess. But after I had paid for two new hood-supports and the repair of a three-foot tear in the hood— somehow I didn't feel so clever.

....

Later on, my Austin was to play a prominent part in another escapade of the type beloved by university students.

A party of motoring friends, having spent a Saturday afternoon watching a motor-cycle trial in the Dublin mountains, had adjourned, full of fresh air, to one of the city's famous eating-houses—the Dolphin Hotel. Here, as on many such an occasion, a very pleasant hour or two was spent over a meal and a tankard of beer, and it is hardly necessary to add that the talk was of motoring and motor sport in all its forms.

Our meal had long been disposed of, and we sat on in an aura of well-being and bonhomie, smoking and drinking and talking.

We were all recounting past exploits and escapades and narrow escapes from the law, and when this topic became exhausted, our thoughts naturally turned to future deeds; and it was at this point that I foolishly mentioned that I had an ambition to cross the Metal Bridge by car.

Again I must pause, for the benefit of those who do not know our capital, to explain what was involved in this peculiar and eccentric, if irrepressible, urge. The Metal Bridge, which has many official and unofficial titles, is a light structure crossing the Liffey almost in the centre of the city, and built solely for the use and convenience of foot traffic; in fact it bears a large notice forbidding even the use of bicycles. It is a narrow affair, led up to on each side by a number of granite steps, and having a steeply arched centre portion. It was originally a toll bridge and bore a charge of one halfpenny to pedestrians, and it is still referred to by old Dubliners as 'the Halfpenny Bridge'.

I had no sooner let slip this secret desire than I regretted it; the boys seized on it as just the sort of outing they were in the mood for. What could be a better time than the present? It was getting late, and Dublin's traffic was thinning out. There were present just the right number of witnesses and collaborators; and the bridge was just round the corner from the hotel.

I was not even consulted as to whether I was serious or not, and a plan of campaign was worked out just as if I was not present. Accordingly, it was arranged that I should park my Austin in a narrow lane near the foot of the bridge; the others would patrol the quays on each side and occupy the attention of any stray policemen or officious citizens. At a given signal on a horn, I was to cross. Just like that.

At my first attempt I misjudged the speed necessary to surmount the steps; the Austin stalled half way up, and I was forced to bump all the way down again backwards. I made no mistake the second time, and was over and bouncing down the steps at the other side before anyone realised what was going on I vanished up a side street and home by devious routes.

It wasn't a particularly clever thing to do, and certainly didn't prove anything; but even now, almost twenty years later, I still have a tiny glow of satisfaction in the knowledge that I was the first—and, I hope, the last—to cross the Metal Bridge by car.

And if any other empty-headed student is tempted by these words to try it, I hope he will think first; it has been done before, and it is Very Bad for a Car.

38

CHAPTER VII.
Reliability Trials

I WAS still a student when I became involved in competitive motoring in the form of reliability trials.

This is a sport which is quite incomprehensible to the ordinary motorist, who is quite naturally under the impression that motor cars were designed to run on roads, and therefore, the better the road, the better the motoring. Why, therefore, he asks, does a certain section of the motoring world spend much time and thought in searching for the worst possible roads and the steepest possible hills and then appear to enjoy thoroughly the sensation of driving on them?

I have often been asked this question by many acquaintances, some of whom were frankly scornful, but for the most part they were genuinely interested. From observation, I should say that 95 per cent of the motoring public have not the slightest idea of what a reliability trial is, and I therefore feel justified in trying to put down on paper some sort of explanation of what goes on, and the reasons for the line of development which modern trials have followed. I make no apologies, but I hope those of my readers who know more about the subject than I do will have patience.

Reliability trials are nearly as old as the motor-propelled vehicle itself. They were first organised by motoring organisations, purely and simply as a means of demonstrating the reliability of this new means of progress—the motor car (or motor-cycle). For the test a longish road journey, with a few mild hills, would be chosen and the winner would be the vehicle which reached the objective with the least delay due to mechanical trouble.

As the motor car improved rapidly, it was found that the majority of entrants would reach the finish without trouble; the length of the course was then increased as the next logical step. Reliability continued to improve, and the courses which sometimes ran into thousands of miles became unwieldy, without making it much easier to find a winner. The next step was to include as many steep hills as possible on the route.

It must be understood that these events were, and still are, run over roads open to the general public; the inclusion of speed, therefore, as part of the test could not be countenanced. In any case, for those who desired speed, racing was being developed, which resulted in the big city-to-city races on the Continent, and ultimately the circuit and track races of to-day. For reliability trials, competitors were asked to average a set speed, which was judged by the organisers to be well within the limits of safety, as well as being inside any legal limit which might be in force at the time. Some other means of finding a winner had to be found, and this involved the selection of a route which would make it impossible to maintain the comparatively low average speed without risk of damage to the machine. Hence the inclusion of rough lanes and almost vertical ascents beloved of the trials driver.

In the past quarter-century, the reliability and sturdiness of the modern machine has reached such a pitch that no course, however difficult, can be found that will not leave a fair proportion of the entry unpenalised at the finish. This has resulted in the inclusion of what is called the 'special test', and it is on the result of such tests that the winner of a trial is usually found.

Special tests have various forms—all designed with devilish ingenuity to upset the calculations of the most impervious driver. One type known as a 'Stop and Restart' involves bringing a car to a stop at a line on the steepest part of a loose-surfaced hill, and then expecting the driver to move off again without rolling back or becoming spin-bound. Another, known as the 'Crossroads Test', consists, roughly speaking, of performing the manoeuvre normally carried out by the ordinary motorist who has taken the wrong road and wishes to turn his car and take the opposite one-—but while being timed by an observer with a stop-watch. In theory, these tests are an excellent means of proving the ability of the driver, and the manoeuvreability of the car. In practice, however, the winner is often found among those who have the nerve to drive backwards round an acute corner at quite abnormal speed, or who are willing to risk bending their axles in broadsiding their cars in narrow, rocky lanes. That this is not always the case is also true, and several trials have been won by staid touring cars, and even saloons, driven by experts who refuse to become flurried when faced by spectators and officials armed with stop-watches.

The foregoing should suffice as an explanation of reliability trials at the stage of development of which I am writing. Later on came the construction of 'trials specials'—cars specially constructed to suit the new courses, but this fascinating study does not come within the scope of these notes.

....

My first trial in the hard-worked little Austin was an event run by the University Club, known as the Joly Cup Trial. In those days there were not many car competitors, and it was the usual practice to include the cars with a motor-cycle entry, and when sections were reached which were quite impracticable for four-wheelers, they were diverted through slightly easier country. In this way the car drivers often had a slight advantage. The Austin proved to be an ideal trials car, being light and manoeuvreable and having ample power for the worst country. The other competing cars were for the most part entirely unsuitable, being under-powered saloons, or retired racing cars—low to the ground and inflexible at low speeds. I should, therefore, be in a position to say that I finished high up in the awards, but unfortunately there is the human element to contend with; I got hopelessly lost in the mountains.

The inability to read a map correctly, and the complete lack of sense of direction have always been a heavy handicap in all my motoring, and particularly in reliability trials, and I would not care to count up in how many such events I have appeared in the results as an 'also started' for this reason. Trials courses are usually marked for the benefit of competitors who are strangers to the district, and this should, in theory, make the following of the correct course an easy matter. The method of marking is to scatter brightly coloured dye on all the corners to be traversed, this being carried out by an official on a motor-cycle, who carries a great number of small paper bags containing the dye. He hurls these bags on the road in such a way that they burst and leave a streak pointing in the correct direction. For many reasons, the system is not infallible; heavy rain before the trial may wash the dye away; mischievous small boys take a delight in scraping up the dye and laying it in another direction, or the marking from a previous event may still be visible after a dry spell. Whatever the reason or excuse, I think I hold the all-time record for Getting Lost in Trials.

When I managed to follow the correct course I sometimes did fairly well, and in the following year I competed for the Joly Cup again, and won this event—I became the temporary proud possessor of my first challenge cup.

Sammy Davis, the author of many books on trials and racing, has said with a great deal of truth that he values his 2nd class awards more highly than his gold medals. His reasoning is this: a cup or gold medal signifies or implies that he has done very well, and therefore has had a trouble-free and uneventful run. But when he looks over his minor awards, they conjure up memories of fighting against great odds, and the overcoming of apparently insuperable difficulties. I would go further still, and say that the events which were most memorable were the ones in which I failed to finish at all. I am reminded of these, not by a small silver award, but by the presence of a crumpled wing or a buckled wheel on the rubbish heap behind my garage.

Such an event comes to my mind now, and I think the story is worth recounting. I had entered my Austin in a trial to be held in the Dublin mountains, and as it was permitted in regulations I invited a college friend to be co-driver. This was by way of a bribe, as it was sometimes difficult to find a suitable passenger who would suffer the rigours of the mountains in winter and the bumping of a trials course without the chance of a turn at the wheel.

All went well until it was my friend's turn to take over. Most drivers are supposed to be bad passengers, but when the car is their own pet they are inclined to become doubly nervous when it is in the hands—even capable hands—of another. Add to this that the owner knows that the car has developed some peculiarities and is liable to dive suddenly to right or left, or to judder sideways off the road—and the situation becomes almost intolerable.

This was the situation on this shared drive, and after I had chewed the upholstery and pressed my brake foot almost through the floor for about ten miles, I could stand no more and insisted on taking the wheel again. At this time we were on the 'Featherbed' road, and about to turn off to descend steeply down a tortuous lane to the aptly named village of Glassamucky; my friend unwillingly and somewhat huffily handed over the wheel.

Whether it was the relief at being back at the controls, or whether I was bent on demonstrating the correct way to handle an Austin, I cannot now say; but the fact remains that we had not gone 200 yards before I found myself approaching a gravel surfaced hairpin about 20 miles an hour too fast. The little car slid into the bank and toppled over into the bog beside the road.

We extricated ourselves, more or less unhurt, and began to inspect the damage, in the hopes of being able to get back on the road and continue, but after a short survey we decided that we had had our trial; all four wheels were buckled, and the wreckage seemed to bristle with spokes like an angry porcupine; the windscreen was shattered, mudguards, lamps and doors seemed to be bent in all directions; the radiator had been pulled clean off at the hose connections.

It took much time and work to turn the car the right way up, and to haul it on to a flat piece of ground. Here we set to work, and after a couple of hours we actually had it standing on four wheels and the engine running again; whether the wheels would support the car in motion was another matter. I don't believe there were enough complete spokes left to make up one proper wheel; one of them, considered serviceable, had five spokes only. When all was ready, we worked the car carefully on to the road and set off gingerly in the direction of Dublin. All went well, but it was found necessary for both driver and passenger to lean far out on the offside—like the crew of a racing yacht in a stiff wind—in order to take the strain off the worst of the wheels. The car had a sort of undulating gait, like the comic motors seen in cinema cartoons.

We had decided that we must head for Trinity College, as I felt I could not face my parents with my car wrecked again. This entailed travelling right through the busiest part of the city, and it is not surprising that we attracted a certain amount of attention. Not only was the car battered almost beyond recognition as such, but it and its crew were covered with blood; not from any serious wound, but in the melee my nose had come in contact with the windscreen, and had started to bleed in the way only noses of the adolescent can. Nothing would stop it, and I had been forced to carry on the work on the car with blood dripping over everything. Horrified gasps and exclamations could be heard as we lurched down Grafton Street and in through the Front Gate of the College. Just as we reached this haven one of the wheels decided it had had enough, and the remaining spokes collapsed; the car subsided on the ground, and had to be dragged to its final resting place.

There were many more trials with the brave little Austin —some successful and some not. They were, of course, packed with incidents highly entertaining to myself, but as they were the type of thing that happen to any trials driver and therefore fairly commonplace, I will not risk boring my reader by relating them.

CHAPTER VIII.
The Organising Side

I WAS not long a member of that small but enthusiastic band, the Dublin University Motor-Cycle and Light Car Club, before I was elected on the committee; in fact I was spotted as the type who would not have the strength of will to resist if the job of Honorary Treasurer was forced on me, and of course I fell for it.

I was soon involved in the organising of both motor car and cycle events; ever since, I have the greatest regard and admiration for the people who go out weekend after weekend to plan and run events in which they cannot hope to compete, and for which work they receive very little in the way of thanks.

To find a suitable trials course means much exploration in little known areas, and the travelling of many miles and the consumption of much petrol. The Trinity College Club was noted for its flair for producing events rather different and more unusual than those run by any other club. In our efforts to keep up this tradition we used to examine the possibilities of the most hair-raising sections and travel to remote parts of the mountains. Very often, my Austin would be used as a sort of 'guinea pig' to see if the sections were practicable. Sometimes they were not.

There is a section well known to motor-cyclists in the Kilbride area, known as Lisheens. Here there are traces to show that a road once existed, which appears to have been swallowed up in a bog. One wet winter we set off for Lisheens to see if it could be incorporated in our next trial. Apart from the fact that there were a couple of inches of water on the surface of the old laneway, it did not look too bad, so I resolutely set the nose of my Austin at it, and hoped for the best. I had proceeded a fair distance and all seemed well—when the car came to a halt, and began to go down by the bows, slowly but surely sinking steadily in the mud. Water and mud began to ooze into the driving compartment, and I decided it was time to abandon ship. It seems that what little foundation there was to the old bog road had vanished at this point, and there was nothing but feet of mud under the wheels, which slowly sank till only the radiator cap was showing above the water. All efforts to move it merely resulted in it going down still further.

None of us were equipped or dressed for this form of rescue work, so there was nothing for it but to retire and think up some plan for extricating the car, and to hope that it would not disappear altogether. Late that evening we returned to the scene, armed with ropes, tackle and sheets of corrugated iron. After much effort, the car proved to be quite immovable, backwards or forwards, so our last plan of campaign was brought into action. Divers went down and fixed the rope firmly amidships; great force was applied, and slowly—with much sucking noise-—the car began to come out, on to its side. Corrugated iron sheets were placed under it and then the operation was repeated from the other side. Slowly the car was hauled over till it was on its wheels again sitting nicely on the iron sheet, mud oozing out from every crack. More sheets were placed behind and the car was dragged back safely on to dry land. Lisheens was not used in our next trial.

Another important function performed by the organisers of a trial is the taking of checks at various points on the route. The checkers have synchronised watches, and they note the arrival and departure times of the competitors; from these figures, along with the results in observed sections, the ultimate awards are decided. Man-power being scarce, it was usual for a checker to see the competitors through one point, and then rush by various short cuts to time them at a point farther on. In some trials, checkers have managed to do duty at three or four checks.

Should a checker fail to arrive at a check point before the competitors, the whole running of the trial would be disrupted, and so many highly exciting races against time were suffered by checkers who had cut things rather fine.

To digress for a moment, there was a story, for the truth of which I cannot vouch, that Tyrrel Smith, the well-known T.T. rider, once organised and competed in a University trial without any assistance whatever. He is credited with having dyed the whole course in the morning; then, having checked all the competitors away at the start, he checked himself out, and by riding like the furies, overtook all the riders and was waiting at the first check to receive them. This was arranged so that he could also observe the competitors and mark their efforts on an observed hill. He then remounted, overtook the field, after 'observing himself' on the hill, and was in time to repeat the performance at the next check—and so on to the finish. The story does not relate what award he gave himself in the final result.

I have in mind an occasion when I, with the aid of another committee member, Harry Carson, and my Austin, had undertaken the responsibility of two checks in a certain trial run by our club. We had allowed plenty of time to get from one point to the other by a short cut, but our calculations were upset as a number of competitors had got lost, or were otherwise in trouble, and had arrived very late at our first control. This left us very little time to take up position some miles away, so we set off at maximum velocity on our somewhat bumpy and narrow short cut.

We were getting on fine, and nearing our destination' which was near the village of Saggart.

Suddenly the car lurched violently and swung into the bank on one side, cannoned off and slid across the road and into the bank on the other side; one more clattering swerve brought it across to the original bank, but about a hundred yards farther down the road. Here it came to rest, and we shakily dismounted to find the cause and examine the damage.
The cause was immediately obvious; a king-pin had fallen out of the near-side front hub. Hub and wheel had disappeared under the car and were trailing along on the end of the track rod. There was not any other apparent damage, so Harry galloped back along the road and with the greatest of luck found the errant king-pin nestling in the grass. It was the work of about two minutes to lift up the car, straighten the track rod, and stuff the king-pin back in its proper place. We set off again, and arrived in Saggart to find only the first two competitors, who were slightly ahead of time, waiting to be checked in.

……………………..

I have explained in previous pages that trials courses were usually marked by an energetic motor-cyclist, who would do so by hurling small paper bags of coloured dye on the road at suitable points. However, it was not always easy to find someone to undertake this rather unpleasant task; it was also rather difficult to explain the route, if it happened to be over new country, and it was a very tiresome business filling some hundreds of little sweet bags with the dye.

When, in preparation for a certain trial, no such willing motor-cyclist could be found, it fell to my lot to lay the trail, with the aid of my Austin. It was at this point that an idea came to my inventive, if perverted, mind. My plan was to make a small hole in the floor of the car, on the passenger's side; we would have a large box of dye in the back of the Austin, and my passenger would be armed with a small scoop of the type used by grocers to measure out flour. When we came to a corner which was to be marked, my assistant would fill his scoop, and pour a little of the dye through the hole in the floor. In this way—I fondly imagined—a line of dye would be plainly marked round the corner, which should leave no doubt as to the correct road to follow. We actually tested this method in the Front Square of the College, much to the disapproval of the authorities.

All went well until we reached the open country. We had not reckoned on a violent and blustery wind, and when the dye was applied to the hole in the floor, instead of pouring out in a nice steady trickle, it was blown back into the car, and over the occupants in a thick blue cloud. It was not long before car and crew were entirely covered in a thick blue layer—and at this point it began to rain.

Not only did this rain effectively fix the dye on all clothing, hair, and upholstery on which it came in contact, but it also completely effaced any little patches of dye which had happened to reach the road—and we were later faced with an angry mob of would-be competitors who had spent the afternoon lost in the mountains.

Since then I have been an ardent supporter of the small paper bag method, dropped on the road by a motor-cyclist.

CHAPTER IX.
Revival of Hill-Climbs

A FORM of motor sport which had fallen out of favour in Ireland at the time of which I write is the speed hill-climb. They were very popular in England, the most notable being the famous event at Shelsley Walsh, and Ulster could boast one classic meeting—at Craigantlet, held in conjunction with the Tourist Trophy races outside Belfast.

For the uninitiated, I must explain that hill-climbing is a type of sport entirely different from both racing and reliability trials. It has a fascination of its own, and develops a type of driving and also—to a certain extent—a type of car suitable only for these events.

Briefly, the idea is this: a piece of road is chosen, varying in length from a few hundred yards to a mile or more. It should have a fairly steep and varying gradient, as many corners as possible, and a good smooth surface. If possible it should have high ground on each side at suitable places to accommodate spectators, and a return road to bring competitors back to the start. Competitors are timed by an accurate electrical device which records the time from the moment the vehicle leaves the starting line until it reaches the finish. They compete singly, one at a time, and have the road to themselves while they are on it.

The type of car suitable for hill-climbs is one that can get away from a standing start and reach a high speed in the shortest possible time. It must also be able to corner well without losing much way, which is difficult to build up again on a steep gradient. Hill-climbing places a high premium on clutch control and gear-changing, as it is here that fractions of seconds are gained or lost, which make so much difference in the results. At the same time, the ordinary sports car can compete on a handicap basis with a fair chance of success and little risk of damage, and because of the shortness of the course the expense due to wear and tear and fuel consumption is small.

The University Club—always out for something new— decided that it was high time that a hill-climb was held in the Dublin area. Accordingly, a small sub-committee was appointed to deal with the matter, and in due course a date was decided on—the first Saturday in the September of 1932. The next step was to find a suitable hill, and this was a matter which took considerable thought and much exploration. The road chosen—apart from being suitable from the competition point of view—would have to be one that did not carry a great deal of traffic, as it would be necessary to obtain permission from the County Council to have it closed to the public for the afternoon. The authorities might be somewhat loth to close a road that might be classed as a main artery. Also it would be necessary to befriend the landowners on each side, in order to have accommodation for spectators at vantage points, and a suitable field for a paddock.

It was eventually decided to use a hill which became known as Mount Venus, not very far from a well-known Dublin landmark, the Hell-Fire Club. About half-a-mile of this road was selected, which included a straight start, followed by a tricky S-bend and then a sharp left turn leading to a straight steep finishing stretch. The road itself was almost ideal, if a little narrow, but the same cannot be said for the spectator accommodation, as there were high hedges on both sides for most of its length.

Having decided on the date and the venue, the work of organising started in earnest, and as is usual when there is work to be done by a small sub-committee, the greatest load all fell on one individual. I need hardly add who that one individual was. Many a day was spent in dealing with the countless problems and tasks which the running of such an event involves; county authorities and police to be seen about the closing of the road; public address and ambulance service to be arranged; poles and ropes for dividing off paddocks; engaging and instructing suitable officials and marshals; advertising and printing of programmes, notices and numbers. Many nights were spent in drawing up the programme and evolving a handicap.

The greatest worry of all confronting us was the finding and encouraging of suitable entrants. We were not troubled for want of support from the motor-cycle fraternity, as these sporting people were always ready for something new and fresh fields to conquer. But the owners of sporting type motor cars seemed to keep them for the purpose of impressing their lady friends, and were rather loth to risk losing their prestige in open competition. Once an event was established, there would be no further difficulty, as competitors who had once tried it would be sure to come along again for more, but we were in the nature of pioneers in this particular form of sport.

Our method of obtaining entries was, perhaps, a little out of the ordinary; we worked on the lines of the naval press-gangs of a bygone age. We would drive round the streets of Dublin, and when we spied anything which had the slightest resemblance to a sports car we would give chase and follow it grimly until it reached its destination, or came to a stop for other reasons. We would then attack the driver, shower him with literature on the subject of hill-climbs and the great merit in competing; we would tell him what a wonderful car he was lucky to possess, and that it was a positive shame to see it wasted in parading the streets of the city when there was a perfectly good hill-climb to compete in.

For the most part, our quarries had not the slightest idea of what we were talking about, and certainly made it clear that they did not intend to become involved in anything so risky to man and machine as a hill-climb, whatever it was. But here and there we came across a man who had always had a secret longing to be a race driver, and these meekly submitted and handed over the entry fee. In this way we collected quite a few names, which, added to the nucleus of enthusiasts who would drive in anything, made quite a respectable showing on the programme. Unfortunately there were some notable absentees, as the Phoenix Park car races were to be held on the following Saturday, and those competing were too busy preparing their cars to have time for our hill-climb.

The great day arrived, and all the officials steadily worked themselves up to a state of nervous apprehension and what is known as 'flap', but little of this appeared on the surface; it was generally agreed that the event was carried through with just the right blend of efficiency and informality which later became the hall-mark of University events. The spectators did not seem to realise the turmoil which was going on in the minds of the organisers as they formed a mental picture of what would happen if the delicate timing apparatus should fail, or the hundred and one other things that might occur. In actual fact everything went smoothly, there were no, accidents, spectators and competitors had an enjoyable day.

Not only did this fixture become an annual one, hut other clubs began to take interest, and many hill-climbs were held in subsequent years. Our little sub-committee felt justifiably proud of having reintroduced this sport in Ireland, and I share in this feeling. But it was this first hill-climb and the preparatory work involved which effectively prevented any thought of serious study during that summer, and was at any rate one of the reasons that my college career was never brought to a successful conclusion.

Although the University Hill-Climb became a traditional annual event, it was not always held on the same road at Mount Venus. As its popularity increased, so did its shortcomings. Owing to the high hedges, it was difficult to keep spectators in a position where they could see anything in reasonable safety. They were inclined to crowd almost to the verge of the rather narrow road, and when a rather wild driver in a 30-98 Vauxhall succeeded in spinning his car completely and thereby almost touching the spectators in doing so the club decided it was time to look for another course. To make matters worse, the local landowners had become antagonistic, owing to the damage done to fences and gates by the large crowds, and just before the third event held there all the fences and hedges were found to be liberally dressed with wet tar. As a further blow, the wires used for the electrical timing device had been cut in several places, and the running of the event had been held up for some time while repairs were made.

A new course was eventually found at Kilternan, on the road to Enniskerry, and here many successful events were held which carried on the University tradition right up to recent years. I did not take a very large part in the organisation of these hill-climbs, as by this time I had become imbued with a desire to be a competitor.

CHAPTER X.

Back to Motor-Cycles

THERE is nothing more exciting and exhilarating than a ride on a good motor-cycle on a fine day.

That is a bald statement of fact which I am prepared to defend against all opposition. But the reader will notice, if he examines the statement carefully, that it includes two qualifying adjectives, both of which are essential to its true interpretation; I could state with almost equal vehemence that there are few things worse than a bad motor-cycle on wet and cold day.

It was not much more than a year after my first motor-cycle had disintegrated when the yearning for another attempt at two-wheeled transport became irresistible and I began to cast round for a suitable machine. I did not have to look very far—in fact I located a possibility less than three miles from my home. I had often noticed the handle-bars of a motorcycle protruding from the heap of scrap and old tyres behind a garage on the main road, and on closer inspection they appeared to be attached to a more-or-less complete machine. I approached the proprietor, who told me I could have it and was welcome to it. I gathered he was glad to see the last of it.

After some time had been spent in removing mountains of scrap of all sorts, the machine was revealed as a 350 c.c. Calthorpe of about 1927, complete in every detail except for a magneto. I was very lucky to discover that the magneto salvaged from my first machine was quite suitable, and in a short time I had the machine running—for a short time. It began to be apparent to me why the machine had been placed on a scrap heap; it would run a minute or two and then seize up solid, and bore signs that it had done this many, many times. However, I had come to possess this machine with absolutely no outlay and I decided it was worth persevering with. I would not look the proverbial gift-horse in the mouth.

The Calthorpe had an entirely inefficient oiling system, and after I had rectified this by the addition of many pipes leading to unoiled parts of the cylinder, I found that it would motor tolerably well. I rode it considerable distances in the mountains and over trials country. It was a very tiring machine to ride, as the frame was very much bent in some bygone crash, with the result that it pulled constantly to one side; in fact, this pull was so pronounced that it was necessary to stop every five miles or so to rest my arms and straighten my back.

It was not long before I was lured into competition, and I entered myself and Calthorpe for what was known as a Go-As-You-Please Trial, run I think by the Tallaght Motor Cycle Club. These trials were an innovation at the time, to suit the beginner in the sport. The idea was that it would not be compulsory to attempt any observed section which the rider might think he would not be able to negotiate. He would lose no marks in by-passing it, but on the other hand, if he attempted it and succeeded he would gain marks, and if he attempted it and failed, he would lose marks. There was no time schedule to be maintained.

Needless to say, I 'had a go' at all the observed sections; I was not unduly worried by the prospect of damage to my machine as were some of the other novices. I was getting on very nicely—much better than I ever expected—and was approaching the final sections when the machine spluttered to a halt for want of petrol. I had to bear the disappointment of seeing the other competitors go on to finish, while I walked disconsolately to the nearest garage.

Imagine my surprise and joy when I read in the papers the next morning that not only was I included in the results, but that I had won the class for veteran motor-cycles. In due course I received a silver ash-tray, suitably inscribed, and I believe I am right in saying that this was an unique award in Irish motor-cycle trials—I had won an event in which I had not finished. The reason was, of course, that I had not been obliged to negotiate the sections which I had missed through lack of petrol, and I had accumulated sufficient marks to beat the others before I fell out.

Later on, I entered this remarkable machine in grass-track races held near Rathfarnham, in a small field on the bank of the River Dodder. This was excellent sport, and I found that the Calthorpe was well-suited to it, as owing to the bent frame, it would go round the left-handed course in great style. I won my heat in the '350 c.c. Standard Tyre Class'— admittedly from a very long handicap. I was just warming up my machine for the final of this event, when there was a loud bang and scrunch from the engine, which became locked as one solid piece of metal. Something terrible had happened inside. I was tasting the depths of despair again, and ready to burst into tears. My disappointment must have showed on my face, because a kindly spectator came forward and offered me the loan of his machine, which happened to comply with the class of my own. I gladly accepted the offer, grabbed the machine and was on the starting line with the others in a matter of seconds. As soon as I started—still carrying the very generous handicap allowance—I realised that the machine under me was far better than my own, and I had no difficulty in winning the final. I am sure the change of machine was highly irregular, but the officials were aware of the circumstances; there were no protests, and I still have a little silver cup to prove it.

I had a theory about motor-cycle trials, which was later borne out in practice by some well-known riders. I averred that the right machine to use was a light-weight, suitably geared down to give sufficient power on rough going.

Unfortunately, my theory did not work out too well in practice when I put it to the test. I had left one important factor out of my calculations—my weight was over 14 stone at the time.

After my Calthorpe had gone to join my first machine in the box in my workshop ignominiously labelled 'Scrap', I started to look round for a machine on which to prove my theory. I eventually came across a little Ariel 250 c.c., shod with 'competition tyres' and offered for the sum of £7 complete. It seemed to be just what I wanted, so I borrowed the £7 and the machine became mine, and I was soon at work getting it into what I thought was a suitable condition for reliability trials. I approached the agents and ordered sprockets which would give me a low enough gear to take me up the worst sections. I took it out and tested it, and was shortly to be found seeing the agent about still lower geared sprockets. By the time I had the gear ratio low enough to take me where I wanted, the engine was making a noise like an angry bee at anything over 20 miles an hour in top gear. It also overheated badly, and I began to lose faith in my theory.

Nevertheless, I entered it in some quite stiff trials in subsequent weeks, and while I got considerable enjoyment and plenty of exercise, I obtained no material reward. Little did I know it at the time, but I was building up a reputation for slowness which was turned to my advantage when, some weeks later, I entered for the University event known as the Rathmichael Scramble. I found myself presented with a positively staggeringly generous handicap allowance. This event was held over some very rough country in the Glencree Valley, and included rocks, bog, river crossings and open heath; there were to be about ten laps of a course measuring about a mile and a half. Being at the top of the handicap, I had the great advantage of not having to pass anybody, while some of the faster men would have to pass me two or three times before they would actually lead me. The little machine buzzed along happily, and I lost all count of the number of laps I had covered. Nobody was more surprised than I when I received the flag to indicate that I had won.

This was my last attempt at competition on two wheels; I think I had at last reached the conclusion that I would never make a motor-cyclist. I have none of the instincts of balance and control and I both feel and look awkward when mounted on a machine. In fact, I often think that the only reason I can drive a car is that it has a wheel at each corner which prevents it from falling over.

CHAPTER XI.
Jock

I CANNOT leave an account of my motor-cycling experiences without referring to my brother, who was much more of a motor-cyclist than I ever hoped to be. Jock entered motor sport at the age of about six, by letting himself coast down through a steep slope in a pine wood in his pedal-car, zigzagging among the trees in such a way that a small error in judgement would mean disaster. He had a keen and mechanical mind, and actually built and ran a petrol-driven car before he reached the age of 13. This machine was a masterpiece of ingenuity, and was driven by a two-stroke engine taken from an auto-cycle which he had brought home 30 miles across the mountains propelled by the pedals alone. The car had four bicycle wheels and the drive was taken through the steering column and gear taken from an old lorry. The machine only travelled about a mile under its own power, but that mile was as earth-shaking to us as the first flight of the Wright Brothers was to the pioneers.

Jock was some nine years younger than I, but he would seldom take my advice on mechanical matters, and I would often find him quietly working away at some idea entirely opposed to standard engineering practice. Sometimes his plans worked out; if they did not, he would cheerfully scrap them and start on something else.

The first motor-cycle which came into my brother's possession was a 1914 model Douglas. I cannot say that either of us actually owned it, because I got it on trial from a college friend with a view to buying—the price being 30/-. The trial lasted so long and was so thorough that the machine had been dismembered long before the purchase price was ever paid. Jock got to work on the machine and proceeded to re-design it in what he considered to be a suitable form for track racing. By the time he had finished with it, it had neither brake nor throttle, clutch nor gears. It had but one control—a magneto cut-out on the handlebar. He then proceeded to make an oval race track in the corner of a wood. It had steeply banked curves and a surface of beaten earth. When it was finished he tried out his machine, and on many an evening he could be seen, tearing round and round, hardly cutting out for the bends, my stop-watch on a string round his neck. After every few laps he would stop to make some adjustment and to note his times—then off again for another test.

'Jock'competing in the University Club's Hill Climb at Kilternan. He won the 350c.c. Hill Climb Championship of Ireland.

- Photo by courtesy 'P.C.' Dublin

Later on, he acquired a 350 c.c. Rudge Whitworth, and succeeded in making this machine go much faster than its makers had intended. He entered it for several races in the Phoenix Park and elsewhere, but was always troubled by pistons which would not stand up to his tuning. The machine shone in short events, however, and he was the holder of the 350 Hill-Climb Championship of Ireland in the face of much more modern competition.

Jock was always trying unusual experiments with a view to bettering the performance of his machine. On one occasion I found him riding his Rudge round and round a field at very high speed and lying in a peculiar upside-down position with his head near the engine. When I came nearer to investigate, I saw that he had in his left hand, believe it or not, an ordinary aneroid barometer of the kind that reads 'Dry—Wet—Stormy'. He had a theory that the atmospheric pressure round the carburettor intake would be low, and he was trying to get a reading on the barometer.

His inventive genius was not entirely confined to his motor-cycles, and when he was living at home, the house became filled with gadgets for opening and shutting doors, turning out lights or automatically letting the cat out. His crowning success was a complete self-change radiogram—a masterpiece of engineering in wire, rubber bands and pieces of Meccano. This machine worked perfectly and would play and change six records. It was, however, rather temperamental and there were one or two jazz records which had a most peculiar effect on it. If one of these discs was inadvertently placed in the machine, it would stop dead, the cabinet door would fly open and records would be hurled out, all over the room.

My brother's career was brought to an abrupt end while he was training for service with the Royal Air Force. There was no man for whom I had a greater regard, and I admired, to the point of envy, his whimsical attitude to life.

CHAPTER XlI.
'Dippy' Harris

OF all my friends in motor sport, there was one who was my constant companion and help, and we shared many a triumph, failure or misfortune in those early, carefree days. This was D. P. Harris, a medical student of about my own age, who inevitably came to be known as 'Dippy'.

We were both obsessed by the same almost fanatical enthusiasm for the sport, but until we met, our interests had followed slightly different lines of expression. I had been content to work away on my own ideas, and the great names in motor racing or the doings of other competitors meant little to me. Dippy, on the other hand, was an avid reader of all the motoring magazines, and had a very full knowledge of every form of the sport. He admired, to the point of hero-worship, the author and racing driver, S. C. H. Davis, and all his books and writings had pride of place on Dippy's bookshelves.

That Harris's practical mechanical knowledge was not as comprehensive as mine was due to circumstances rather than to lack of ability. He lived in rooms in college, and therefore was without workshop or garage; if he wished to take his car to pieces he had to do so in the open spaces of Botany Bay —an exceedingly uncomfortable operation.

The car that was Dippy's pride and joy (and torment) was an ancient Riley tourer, which he had so altered from the maker's specification as slightly to resemble a sports car of the period. It was known as 'Roarin' Meg', and indeed the enormous exhaust pipe which protruded from the rear resembled and sounded like the famous Londonderry cannon of that name. It was fitted with all the paraphernalia considered essential on the best racing cars—skimpy front mudguards, a large strap round the bonnet, and extra large filler caps on the radiator and petrol tank. As the machine had been manufactured in the age of beaded-edge tyres, and long before front wheel brakes had been thought of, its performance belied its sporting appearance; but it was, on the whole, a fairly reliable car and it gave its owner and myself many miles of pleasurable motoring, including some competition work.

I had not known Dippy very long when he invited me to share the driving in the next Ulster Rally, in which he intended to enter Roarin' Meg. Needless to say, I accepted with alacrity and we were soon hard at work preparing the car for this fairly stiff event. The Rally was a run of about 800 miles which covered most parts of Ireland and was arranged to finish in Bangor, near Belfast, a few days before the Tourist Trophy races. There was also a Concours d'Elegance, in which we were obviously not interested.

'Dippy' Harris in the Frazer Nash pits at the 1933 Ards TT race

We managed to get the Riley into a fairly roadworthy condition—except in one important respect. The tyres were very old, very worn, and rather liable to fly off if corners were not treated with great care. There were no better tyres available at the price we were prepared to offer, so we resigned ourselves to the likelihood of a good deal of trouble, and were carrying a good supply of gaiters, patching, solution, and tyre-levers. Then, at the very last moment, less than half an hour before we were due to start, a certain friend, owner of a small garage, arrived with a set of part-worn tyres and offered them to us at a very small figure, and what was better, he was prepared to wait until after the Rally to receive payment. We accepted the offer, and began to fit the tyres at the side of the road where the Rally was due to start in a few minutes. So while the remainder of the competitors were lounging about, awaiting their starting times beside their perfectly prepared cars, we were working like blacks with pump, tyre-levers, and jack. The task was completed just in time, and we set off on the long journey, with the feeling that we had had quite enough wheel-changing to last us for some time.

Owing to the comparatively mild performance of the old Riley, it was necessary to drive it at almost its maximum speed in order to maintain the 30 miles per hour average which was set for the Rally. The car ran very steadily, however, and we found that we had sufficient time to spare at some of the checks to grab a hasty meal without penalty. We had decided to share the driving by changing over at alternate checks, and this arrangement worked very well until the late evening of the first day. It happened to be my turn at the wheel, when darkness began to envelop the countryside, and I reckoned I had about a couple of hours to do by the light of the headlamps. I switched on and settled down to some high-speed night driving.

All went well for a few miles, and then, as we hit a bad patch of road, there was a blinding flash—and all the lights went out. A short halt for examination showed that the jolt had shaken the connections from the battery, and the full voltage of the dynamo had been transmitted direct to the lamps, which had flared up and burnt out the filaments.

Needless to say, we had no spare bulbs, so we had the alternative of retiring then and there or of making some attempt to carry on handicapped by a complete lack of illumination. We chose the latter.

At the moment we came to this decision, while we were still standing at the roadside, we were passed by a competitor in a small car whose speed, we reckoned, would not be much greater than our own. In a second we had jumped in the Riley and were in hot pursuit, and having caught up, we tucked in close behind with the intention of tailing it throughout the night. The leading car had good lights and the task was not as difficult as I had imagined; in fact, when our guide was passed by a slightly faster car we abandoned him and proceeded to tail the new leading light.

It is much easier to follow another car at night in strange country, even without lights, than it is to lead the procession, as the leading car will give ample warning of any corner or other obstruction which may be encountered. The result was that we made several changes of guide during the long night, and when dawn broke we were far ahead of our time schedule. In fact, I think we were the third car to arrive at the first check of that early morning in the wilds of Donegal.

Though we had planned to change drivers at every check, it had not been possible to do so during the night, as we could not risk losing our guides and being left alone without lights or any idea as to our position. I was therefore glad when the morning came and I was relieved of the strain for a few hours.

The second day of the Rally proved to be a real 'scorcher' and the sun beat down on us unmercifully as we sped along the dusty country roads of the north-west of Ireland. My turn at the wheel came round during the hot afternoon, and my passenger relapsed in deep sleep in the seat beside me. Dippy had an amazing capacity for sleeping in uncomfortable conditions, and he was now lying back with his unshaven face burnt a brick red and his mouth wide open, exposed to the full force of the sun and wind. While he lolled in this grotesque attitude, I drove on and passed through several towns, and even stopped to ask the way from incredulous townsfolk who were too awestruck by the sight to be able to give a coherent answer.

We reached the final control that evening, tired, dirty, but happy in having covered the whole distance without loss of marks. Our pleasurable feelings were somewhat damped, however, when we were confronted with the test that was to decide the eventual winner of the Rally.

A portion of the main street of the holiday resort of Bangor had been roped off. White lines had been painted on the road, and gaily painted marker flags waved in the breeze. The whole population of the town had turned out to watch in critical silence this final exhibition. It was a Brake Test.

Now, the brakes of Roarin' Meg, which acted only on the rear wheels, were in the ordinary way, to say the least, somewhat mild; but after 800 miles all over lreland, there seemed to be no appreciable difference to her progress whether they were on or off.

As car after car drove up to the indicated stopping place, and with a sudden shriek of tyres on tarmac, stopped in what appeared to be about half its length, we became more and more apprehensive. When our turn eventually came, Dippy came into the arena and headed Meg for the stopping line at the required approximate speed of 30 miles per hour. Meg sailed majestically up to the line, and Dippy slammed on the brakes. Meg continued to sail on majestically.

The Riley relentlessly continued on its way, through the Braking Area and on towards where the organisers had considered it safe for the watching public to stand. At the last moment, the crowd opened a narrow alleyway to let the car through, and Meg proceeded on her way towards the sea, to come to rest quietly and unassumingly in a deserted part of the town.

No, we did not win any prizes, but Roarin' Meg proudly carried for the rest of her days a little plaque on the dashboard, presented by the Ulster Automobile Club, to indicate that she had finished in the Ulster Rally.

CHAPTER XIII.
The Beginning of the Chain Gang Era

ROARIN' MEG, as mentioned in the previous chapter, while being an admirable car in many ways, had somewhat mild speed capabilities; she was therefore entirely unsuitable for hill-climbs, sprints or competition of any kind where speed was the important attribute; her otherwise proud owner was fully conscious of this shortcoming, and as he was determined to take part in speed events, he conceived the idea of building what is known as a 'special'.

Dippy Harris, having followed closely the reports of hill-climbs and speed events which were very popular in England at the time, was very well informed as to the types of car taking part. He was particularly enthusiastic about the performance of the home-made cars known as Shelsley Specials—machines constructed by amateurs, and mainly designed to compete at the Shelsley Walsh Hill-Climb—and it was not long before he had infused into me the same urge to build.

The basis on which most of these curious and exciting machines were formed was the old chain drive two cylinder G.N. cycle-car, so when Dippy heard that there was one of these models lying in the open behind a house in Monkstown, he lost no time in asking me to come with him to inspect it.

I must say, when I saw this car, I was rather disappointed, and I found it difficult to visualise this high, spidery vehicle converted into a racing machine. However, Dippy said he knew exactly all the alterations that should be made, and as the car seemed to be in reasonable condition, that is to say, there was an engine and four wheels with tyres on them—we decided to buy if the price was not excessive. The owner turned out to be quite amenable, and the G.N. changed hands for the sum of two pounds cash; in a short time it was attached to the back of the Riley, and we set out on the long tow home.

It was an uneventful journey, though quite exciting as the G.N. had practically no brakes; but as the Riley had no brakes either, there was no great danger of running into the back of it. Our new machine seemed very high and light after anything else that I was used to, and it took some time to become accustomed to the small wheel and very direct steering gear.

The first GN acquired and basis for 'The Horror'.

We arrived at my home near Dublin, where it had been decided we would keep our new acquisition. Here there was an old shed where we could work under cover, and I had a fairly comprehensive set of tools which would be useful in the big reconstruction.

The next day, we started work early, and began to remove all non-essential equipment, such as mudguards, windscreen, and tattered hood. The desire to try out the engine became irresistible, so we filled up with petrol, and after much towing and pushing the two cylinders began to fire in a rather desultory manner, but sufficiently well to demonstrate that the car would actually move under its own power. We spent the rest of the day making adjustments, and towards evening we had it going well enough to take it out on the road for a trial. The idea was to gauge its performance in its present condition, so that we could later judge the effect of our tuning. The real reason was that we could not resist the temptation to go for a spin in this strange machine.

We set off on a trip in the Dublin hills—a circuit of about 20 miles. The engine spluttered and thumped along cheerfully at about 40 miles an hour, and we quickly got used to the rather intricate gear-change and the peculiar cornering, due to the 'solid' rear axle. As we neared home and the dusk was gathering into darkness, we were amazed to see both cylinder heads, which protruded through the bonnet on each side, glowing red hot. In fact, they were so hot that they had a sort of translucent appearance, and we could almost imagine that we could see the pistons working up and down inside. I have never discovered if this was a normal phenomenon in this type of air-cooled engine; it certainly didn't make much difference to the running, and we got home safely.

The next few weeks were spent in dismantling the G.N. completely, and then the slow business of rebuilding and tuning started in earnest. In the meantime Dippy had visited Belfast, where he had located most of another G.N. This car had one wheel missing, so Harris, having bought it for 30/-, had brought the car to Dublin by lifting the whole front end on to the back of his Riley, so that it travelled on two wheels only. I believe the Customs Officers at the Border were rather puzzled when he presented for export a four-wheeled vehicle, on which he could only account for three wheels.

We were now in a stronger position, as we had a supply of spare parts. Our special began to take shape, and we found that most of the parts were very adaptable and it was not a difficult job to rearrange everything to give the car a lower and more sturdy appearance. The engine also received a certain amount of attention, but of course we could not indulge in super-tuning without the very special equipment necessary.

The chassis of the G.N. rather resembled the ordinary iron bedstead; there could be no simpler design. Many of our English contemporaries, whose ideas we were following, were in the habit of running their cars completely devoid of any form of coachwork, and on account of this, they were often nicknamed 'Flying Bedsteads'. We, in our small way, intended to imitate this fashion; at least, we intended to test our car thoroughly before we would go to the expense of building a body.

Up to this point in my narrative I have endeavoured as far as possible to avoid technicalities. But now— confronted as I am with this peculiar and unorthodox mass of machinery— I find I can go no further without some explanations which must be, by their very nature, slightly technical. Even the title of this chapter cannot he passed over without some comment on a mechanical theme. I reckon that any reader who has been sufficiently interested to come so far with me will have the type of mind for which I am writing and will not be disconcerted by my attempts to describe the fascination of the G.N. I can do no more than apologise to those readers who may be looking for purely human interest.

The G.N. car which we had chosen for a basis for our special had several unique features, the main ones being the method of driving the back wheels and of changing gear. The drive from the engine was taken by a shaft to a bevel gear and counter-shaft situated under the driving seat, and from there the power was transmitted to the back axle by a row of chains, one of which operated each gear. In fact, the appearance of the back end of the car when exposed to the eye gave the impression of a mass of whirling chains. Hence, owners of G.N.s, and later on, the owners of Frazer Nashes which were developed from them, became known as members of the 'chain gang' and took a peculiar pride in being so classified. These chains were quite satisfactory if in reasonable condition, but occasionally they would break and fly off, so it was considered advisable to have some form of armour plating between them and the seat of the occupants. It was also possible, if the right adjustments were not made, to engage two gears at once, when the most disastrous things would happen to the whole transmission—as we were to learn several times before we discovered the remedy.

A weak point in the design was the method for fixing on the wheels. They were held on by a form of centre nut, which in turn was supposed to be prevented from unscrewing by a small locking device. Very often this device would fail to perform its function, the centre nut would unscrew and the wheel would fall off. The number of times this happened was countless, and I remember losing three different wheels on a 100-mile trip from Dublin to Limerick. However, the car was so low to the ground that the loss of a wheel was hardly noticeable, and it was only the matter of a few minutes to retrieve the wheel and refit it.

The work of rebuilding had gone on apace, and we soon reached the stage when the car, although by no means finished, was ready to test. We found ourselves unable to resist the temptation to try out the result of our labours, and this impatience very nearly resulted in disaster.

We had always found that, while the car was partly dismantled, we could work away, steadily and methodically, with no great longing for the time when we could try it out. But when the car was standing on all four wheels, with oil in the engine and petrol in the tank, attention to detail became very scant, and the necessity of such things as tightening on the steering wheel would be over-ruled by the overpowering urge to sample the acceleration.

Discretion having yielded to enthusiasm, we wheeled the machine out of its shed and into the lane. It would have to be started by pushing, as we had not arranged for any other method. Dippy sat on the piece of board which served as a seat, and I pushed with all my might, but apart from a few coughs and splutters, nothing happened.

It was decided that we would both have to push, so it was arranged that Dippy should run alongside, and at the right moment would shove the gear lever into second gear. If it started, he would jump aboard and take control.

The plan was put into operation; we both pushed mightily; in went the gear—and away went the G.N. It seems the throttle was open wider than we had thought, and as soon as the engine fired the car dived forward, leaving Dippy nothing to hold but the gear lever. We had a vision of our precious car wrecking itself against a tree, and then Dippy gathered himself and took a flying leap into the midst of the machinery. A quick wriggle and he was on the piece of board and in control, but from where I stood I could see the seat of his trousers circulating rapidly among the chains.

Although the car was now more or less under control, the driver found that he was quite unable to bring it to a stop or to reduce its speed. He found he could not get it out of gear, and in our anxiety to get it going we had quite forgotten to connect the brakes, and the fitting of an ignition switch had just not occurred to us. Dippy turned into an open field and proceeded to circle it. The only control within reach which would help him to stop was the petrol tap; he turned it off and continued to circle the field, while the remains of the seat of his trousers were slowly reduced to shreds among the whirling chains.

This experience acted as a slight deterrent, and we did not take the car out again until we had all the controls working in a more or less efficient manner.

When we eventually got the car out for prolonged tests, we were to be disappointed at the performance of the engine. It certainly was better than when we had first acquired it, but it was a long way from the high-efficiency racing engine which we imagined we were producing. We also found that, in producing more speed, we had sacrificed reliability, and in this respect we had a good deal of trouble.

Testing the first 'Horror'

This engine was a two-cylinder air-cooled affair, so arranged that one cylinder stuck out through the bonnet at a jaunty angle on each side. It had side exhaust valves and overhead inlet valves which were operated by long push rods, and it was these that gave us most trouble. If the engine was speeded up to more than its accustomed revolutions per minute, the push rods would fly out like arrows, and would disappear over the hedges into the surrounding countryside. Much time was spent in fruitless search for the errant rods, and Dippy suggested that we should carry a quiverful of spare ones for use in emergencies. We never discovered a solution to the problem of how to keep them in place, but losses were reduced by attaching each push rod to the car by a long piece of string, so that they could be retrieved before they went too far. This was not the only weak point in the engine, and it was not long before our thoughts turned to the possibility of obtaining a more orthodox power unit.

In the meantime, the date for the second Mount Venus Hill-Climb was getting near and it was decided to run the G.N. as it was, and to hope for a good handicap. I was down to drive in the first event, and I brought the car to the line, barking and popping in true G.N. style. I made quite a good start, but when I tried to change from first to second gear the nervous tension must have caused me to overdo this delicate operation. There was a grinding scrunch, and the car came to a shuddering halt, not a hundred yards from the start. One glance at the rear portion was enough to show that two gears had become engaged at once, and the transmission was now a tangled mass of bent shafts and twisted chains. So ended our first attempt at a speed event.

The G.N. was completely immovable, and had to be carried by brute force off the road. Later on we tackled the job of sorting out the chains, and after further investigation it was found that the worst of the damage was a bent countershaft and slightly bent back axle. We replaced the chains, and found that the car would actually run, but in a highly unusual manner. The bent countershaft caused the bevel box to have a peculiar circular movement, and as this component was directly under the seat, the motion was transmitted to it, and thence to the occupant, who would find himself bobbing up and down about 150 times a minute with the engine running slow. We attempted to drive home in this way, but after about a mile my stomach began to protest at this treatment; we took off the chains again and the rest of the journey was accomplished sedately at the end of a tow rope.

A 10 H.P. Rover engine is fitted

A complete rebuild was obviously necessary, and now was the time to go into the question of another power unit. We started to look round for a suitable engine and much time was spent searching through the scrap-yards. The one place we did not investigate, naturally enough, was my own garage; and yet it was from here that our new engine came.

My father had been in failing health for some time, and it was many months since he had driven a car; in fact, it was unlikely that he would ever be fit enough to drive again. In the garage, therefore, was his car, gathering dust and rust—a pure waste of a good little machine, or so it seemed to us at the time. It was a Rover Ten, only a couple of years old, and having a very lively overhead valve engine, exactly the kind of power unit we were looking for.

At first, the idea of taking the engine from this car seemed preposterous—a thing we wouldn't dream of doing. But the more we tried to forget the idea, the more we thought about it. Just as a matter of interest we measured it one evening —and found that it would fit in our chassis as if made for it. This made it still harder to banish the wicked thought.

Then, late one night when the madness was full on us, we silently went to work. In the morning the Rover was to all outward appearance exactly as before; but if anyone had opened the bonnet, he would have seen nothing but a vacant space.

We salved our consciences by telling ourselves that if the Rover was ever required, it would be a simple matter to buy a secondhand engine and to put it in running order again. (This was, in fact, done some time later. An engine was found and installed, and the car was sold at a quite satisfactory price.)

The winter was spent in fitting the Rover engine, and in rebuilding the transmission of the G.N. When spring came the job was nearly complete, and we were satisfied that we now had a special with real possibilities. We had not yet reached the stage of fitting a body, and we were determined to run it in one or two events in its naked form to prove its capabilities.

Specials of the type we were building when competing in England were usually endowed with picturesque names, such as 'Spider', 'Bloody Mary', 'The Terror', or 'Dorcas'. This latter was a biblical character who, you may remember, was a woman 'full of good works'. We decided that our machine must also have a name, and it was duly christened 'The Horror'.

The first event on the sporting calendar was a hill-climb to be held at a new venue—De Selby Hill, and we determined to enter the 'Horror' in its present form.

One evening we went out to this hill, which was not very far from my home, for a little unofficial practice. On our first trip up the hill we noticed a large hole in a stone wall which we did not remember having observed before. We stopped to investigate, and were amazed to see, in the field beyond the hole, the wreckage of what had once been a racing car. Standing disconsolately beside the pieces was the figure of Wilford Fitzsimmons, a driver who later became very well known for his successes in reliability trials.

The car, which Wilford had brought to the hill for the same reason as ourselves, was a special, somewhat akin to our own, and afflicted with the same narrow beaded edge tyres.

It was built very low, and owing to the close proximity of the drive shaft to the person of the driver, it had a Very Rude Name. It appeared that one of the tyres had parted company with its wheel while the car was descending the hill, and it had left the road via the wall, and it was now in a condition to require no further dismantling. Curiously enough, later on a number of its parts became incorporated in the 'Horror'.

At this time I found myself on the horns of a dilemma. I had been offered a place in the University boat which was to compete in the Head of the River race at Putney, and the date coincided with the day of the De Selby Hill-Climb. After much mental strife, I decided I must go to London with the crew, and so Dippy Harris was left to run the 'Horror' at home. That he did so with some success was no little consolation to me. It appears that the car caused quite a sensation, and I still treasure the telegram which I received in my hotel in London that night. It read, 'HORROR PLACED FIRST IN TWO EVENTS. LOVE DIPPY'.

We were now satisfied that our special was a success, and we decided it was worthy of a little coachwork. Dippy and I had rather divergent ideas on what the body should look like; he was all for graceful curves and a streamlined tail, while I, sensitive to our lack of the panel-beater's skill, was all for the short, squarish style which had been adopted by the M.G. concern, and which is quite modish even to-day. In the end we produced a rather odd-looking square body, which looked quite well when the spare wheel was in place to cover up the bareness of the tail.

Our car, which could now be classed as a true racing machine, had some unique features which I have not so far described I think they will be of interest to the technically minded reader, and also to others who may be in search of the bizarre.

When we fitted the Rover engine, we also fitted the gearbox which went with it. This implies that the car now had two gear-boxes, and two gear-levers. A little mechanical musing will now show that we had a wonderful combination of gears—to be exact, 13 forward speeds and seven reverse gears. This is accounted for as follows: the Rover gear-box had four speeds and reverse, and the G.N. arrangement provided for three forward and a reverse. One could therefore put

'Horror' at speed on De Selby Hill-Climb

available gears in the other—and so on. The thirteenth gear, you query? Put both gear-levers in reverse, and the car would move forward, but very, very slowly.

In actual fact, all these gears were of purely academic interest, the Rover gear-box was normally left in top gear, and all changes were made with the G.N. system. But a great deal of fun could be had by demonstrating the vehicle before incredulous audiences; the car would be put in its lowest gear and left to itself with the engine ticking over. Under these conditions its forward motion could only be detected by careful scrutiny, and it would take several minutes to move a few yards.

Another peculiarity was the steering. If the wheel was turned beyond full lock the steering would reverse itself so that a turn of the wheel in one direction would cause the car to circle in the opposite direction. Great hilarity could be caused by getting a stranger to drive it in an open space with the steering so reversed, and watching his efforts to make the car go where he wanted.

CHAPTER XIV.
A Trip to Tramore

AS our car was now running to our satisfaction, we started to look round for events in which to compete, and it was not long before we got wind of a suitable fixture which was to take place in the South of Ireland. The annual sand races were to be held at Tramore.

This was just the sort of event that would suit the G.N., so we lost no time in submitting our entry, and started to prepare the car for the trip. As I have remarked before, sand racing is a sport that is only indulged in by the maddest enthusiasts, because of the awful things that sand and sea water can do to the inside of a car, but the reader of these notes will have classed us in this group by now.

The 'Horror' was not taxed to run on the road under its own power, so we planned to tow it down behind Harris's Riley, 'Roarin' Meg'. Neither of us relished the idea of being towed 120 miles in the G.N., so I set to work to design a tow bar which would both pull and steer the car when under tow. After a considerable amount of trial and error I evolved a satisfactory system, which we tried out near home; it was fascinating to watch the unoccupied racer following faithfully behind. With this arrangement we could both travel in comfort in the Riley, and also we found we could stow a good deal of our equipment in the cockpit of the G.N.

We decided to go down to Tramore on the day before the event, to give us plenty of time to prepare the car and to examine the course, and perhaps to do a little practice on the sand. We set off at a moderate pace, out of respect for our precious G.N., and because we were in no particular hurry, and it was a lovely day. It was amusing to see the expressions on the faces of other motorists as they passed our unusual cavalcade—the driverless, bright-red G.N. following the only slightly less garish Riley. Now and then other entrants for the races would flash by on their way to Tramore, and would give us a cheery wave.

'Horror en route to Tramore behind 'Roarin' Meg'

It was when we were descending a gentle hill on a straight portion of the main road that an incident occurred—an incident of the kind that always seemed to happen just when our little expeditions were becoming slightly humdrum.

Dippy, who was driving, had been keeping one eye on his driving mirror, as we were expecting more entrants for the races to pass us on the road. Suddenly he exclaimed, "Hello, here's an unusual red car coming up behind."

Sure enough, a low red car swished past us and went on ahead. Then, with a simultaneous gasp, we both realised the truth. As one voice we shouted: "It's the 'Horror'."

Holding our breath, we watched the careering, driverless car—and awaited the inevitable crash.

As luck would have it, the road was straight and level; there was no other traffic. The 'Horror' gently drifted with the camber until the nearside wheels were in the gutter. Then, running as if on rails, the car gradually slowed and came to a halt, unshaken and unscathed.

When we had recovered our breath, we shakily dismounted and examined my patent towing bar. Everything was in order, except for one bolt, which I had not bothered to secure by a split-pin. This bolt had unscrewed itself and had fallen out, and as I looked the dreadful thought of what might have happened through this little bit of carelessness hit me very forcibly. Since that day we have always attached an ordinary tow-rope when using the self-towing bar, as an additional safety precaution.

The rest of the journey was uneventful, and we arrived at Tramore with time in hand to try the car out on the sand before darkness fell. In a very short time we had the car unhitched and our gear unloaded, and we pushed the G.N. down the slipway on to the level stretch of hard sand.

We could see that it was going to be difficult to put in any real practice, because half the holiday population of the little resort seemed to be spread over the fairway, intent on enjoying the last rays of the setting sun. However, we started the engine and, carefully weaving in and out among the deck chairs and sand castles, we made for a fairly clear spot at the far end of the beach. Here we increased speed and Dippy, who was driving, decided to try a fast turn. Choosing a piece of sea-weed as a marker, he pulled the car round in what he imagined would be a suitable style for sand racing.

There were three loud bangs in rapid succession—and the 'Horror' came to a lurching halt. Three tyres had pulled off the rims—the inner tubes burst.

We were now about a mile from our base—the Riley, on a deserted part of the beach. The tide was coming in, and we had heard of the terrible things that happen to a car that is left for long on one spot on the porous sand. So with a great effort we got the engine started, and drove it, limping, to a point just above the high tide mark. Then we set out for a weary walk back along the sands towards the twinkling lights of Tramore. Here we were in luck, and having located the principal garage, the proprietor was able to produce three motor-cycle inner tubes, which, although not strictly the right size for our car, would be near enough to suit. We then collected all the necessary gear for tyre changing from the Riley, and trudged back to the abandoned racer.

Changing tyres at any time is not my idea of fun; but when three tyres have to be changed, pumped and fitted, working in the dark and on soft, powdery sand—well, anyone can have my share.

The job was eventually finished, and we decided that we could just drive the car back to the town on the thin strip of firm sand still showing between the advancing tide and the soft dunes. This done, we hitched the 'Horror' to the Riley and prepared to take our impedimenta to a less conspicuous spot than the sea front of Tramore.

We had set out on this trip with no thought of where or how we were going to spend our nights; we could not afford hotels even if there was any possibility of finding rooms in the height of the season. We were now too tired to care where we slept, and as the night was fairly fine we decided to drive out into the country and to make a camp at the first suitable spot.

Having made up our minds, we left Tramore behind us and set off inland, and we had not travelled more than a couple of miles when we saw an ideal camp site right beside the road—a green level patch, protected by a low wall, and overhung by a shady tree. We pulled the convoy close in to the wall, and began to prepare for the night.

Now, Dippy and I were not what might be termed 'old campaigners'; our ideas on how to make a camp would not have gained us first-class badges in the Boy Scouts. Dippy's ideas were simple; having pulled the Riley close in to the wall, he proceeded to throw everything movable overboard on to the grass. Then, when we had partaken of a frugal meal of chocolate and fruit, he wrapped himself in rugs and coats and retired, to sleep full-length in the car. I thought I would prefer the open spaces and the comparative softness of mother earth, so I stretched myself, equally well wrapped up, in a spot where I hoped to benefit to a small extent from the heat of the still warm radiator.

To sleep in these conditions was not as easy as we had thought, tired out though we were; there were to be several interruptions to the peace of the summer night.

When we had chosen our camp site, we had not noticed that we were situated on a slight bend—on the main road between Tramore and the neighbouring city of Waterford. Even in the small hours of the morning, this road was by no means infrequently used.

This fact was brought home to us soon after we had settled down for the night, when we found ourselves bathed in the bright stage-like light of approaching headlights. There was a squeal of brakes as the late travellers braked to avoid what must have looked like a particularly bad road accident—two cars locked close together against a wall, and the ground covered with wheels, seats, and even a recumbent body. There was a silent pause—as though the driver had become petrified by the terrible scene, and then the car was restarted and tore away into the night, as though the occupants were determined to get as far away as possible in the shortest possible time.

We had hardly settled down again, when the same performance was repeated—the bright, theatrical illumination, the squeal of brakes, the short silence, and the car receding rapidly in the distance.

Late in the night I managed to slip into uneasy slumber; at least I think I must have dropped off, because I found myself coming back to consciousness to feel the cold patter of rain on my face.

Dismally I looked round for possible shelter, and my eye fell on the faintly discernible bonnet of our precious racer. It was a single-piece affair of sheet metal, and it struck me instantly that here was an ideal bivouac. I was in no mood to think of wet magnetos and carburettors, and it was the work of a minute to take off the bonnet and to arrange it tent-wise on the ground.

I crawled inside, and was soon lulled to sleep by the gentle drumming of the rain on my 'tin roof'.

The rest of the night was more or less undisturbed, and it was very early morning when we were finally roused from further hope of sleep by the stertorous blowing of a small herd of inquisitive cows, nuzzling among our effects as they sauntered on their way up the road to pastures new. Dirty and hungry, we packed our gear back in the cars, and set out for Tramore again, and made straight for the largest hotel, where we demanded a wash and a large breakfast from the scandalised and scarcely awake staff.

The morning was spent in going over the car carefully, and preparing it for the coming race. We met several other competitors engrossed in the same task, and there was a good deal of the usual pre-race chatter. We were lucky to meet a man who had a fair knowledge of sand-racing, and it was from him that we got a valuable tip on the thorny question of how to keep the tyres on the rims when making the fast, semi-broadsiding turns on the sand. He said, pump them up about twice normal pressure and they should stay on. We were very glad of this advice as, after our experience of the night before, we had grave doubts of ever finishing the race.

Sand-racing is a peculiar sport, in that the time at which the event takes place is governed more by the whims of nature than by the designs of mankind. Accurate tide-tables are carefully drawn up, but wind and weather affect the actual time that the tide stays sufficiently far out to allow the programme to be carried through to schedule. Also, the condition of the sand varies so much from tide to tide that the location and length of the course cannot be decided until shortly before the event.

On this particular day the tide receded to leave a fine level surface with only one or two wet patches. The paddock area, however, was rather waterlogged, and the cars which occupied it had to be moved at frequent intervals to prevent them from sinking to the axles in the sand.

Final preparation at Tramore

As the time for the race to start drew near we brought the 'Horror' out to the paddock, and it was only then that we were handed a programme of the runners and showing the allotted handicaps.. We were amazed to see that we had been classed among the fastest cars—in fact, we had the same handicap as a 30-98 Vauxhall and a well-known special racing Ford from Kilkenny.

It seems that when we had filled in our entry form we had not been too explicit as to the possible performance of our car, and we had used the magic word 'special'. This, to the local committee at Tramore, signified something likely to go very fast, and as they were not going to take the chance of a runaway win, they put us down near the bottom of the list. And so, as we were directed to our position on the starting line, we knew that we had very little hope of doing more than finishing in this, our first sand-race. We were not in the least depressed, however, as the possibility of a win or even a place had never really entered our minds.

All was now ready for the start, and a local worthy strode out to the head of the line. With a flourish of the starting flag he sent the first group of slower cars away on the 30-mile journey, and at varying intervals the progressively faster cars were sent off. Soon our turn came, and at the drop of the flag there was a roar as the three vastly different cars shot off the line.

We considered we had made a good start, but the Ford and the Vauxhall were 200 yards ahead as we approached the first flag-marked turn.

Dippy, who was driving, decided to take the turns cautiously at first, as he had no experience on the sand, and also we were rather doubtful of the ability of the old tyres to stay on the rims; nevertheless, the car seemed to handle well, and it was a delightful sensation, swinging round the bend on the billiard table surface of the almost virgin sand. We covered two or three laps at our own speed and then, as all was going well and the engine running happily, we started to open up.

The flying sand thrown up by the unprotected front wheels began to beat on our faces like hail, and we could understand why the more experienced drivers had fitted small front mudguards; the sea water from the soft patches on the seaward leg of the oval course soon drenched us to the skin. Now and then a faster car roared past, covering us in its spray and wake of flying sand. Occasionally—very occasionally—we caught up on a slower car, and were smothered in wet sand before we left it behind.

In spite of the minor discomforts, we were thoroughly enjoying ourselves. We were competing in a real race at last.

As the surface of the turns began to break up, our little car was getting heavy punishment. Dippy, however, was enjoying himself and was going in to the turns with more and more verve. I was just about to shout in his ear that it might be well to ease up a bit when there was a loud bang, the car lurched wildly, and a rear tyre left us and rolled rapidly out towards the advancing tide.

In a second we were out of the car, the axle was hoisted on to our quick-action jack, wheel removed, spare wheel fitted— and we were back in the race, and going harder than ever.

Whatever may be said about the liability of the G.N. wheels to fall off, they were certainly very easy to remove and replace; we heard afterwards that we had made the quickest wheel-change ever seen at Tramore.

For another couple of laps everything went well, but the pace was beginning to tell. The amount of sand thrown over the chain gear of the 'Horror' was causing a rough grinding sound, and the clogged gear-lever became more and more difficult to move. Around the course we could see many other competitors in trouble; some had lost

'Dippy' and the author enjoying the sand racing at Tramore.

tyres like ourselves, others were suffering from water in the ignition, as they dashed through the waterlogged sand on the seaward stretch of the course, where the tide was now advancing rapidly.

Suddenly I became aware of a strong smell of burning rubber, which was definitely coming from our car. I could think of no reason for this, as there was no electrical equipment, and no rubber fittings anywhere near the exhaust system. I looked round for a possible cause, and my eye fell on the offside rear tyre. It was ringed with a haze of blue smoke and steam, and frayed rubber was flying off in small pieces; in fact, it looked as if it was about to disintegrate at any moment. I had never seen anything like this before, and was quite at a loss to explain the phenomenon.

I shouted to Dippy and pointed at the steaming tyre, but even as I did so I noticed that it seemed to be cooling off, and after a short time the wheel was running normally, if somewhat frayed.

At the very next turn, we had forgotten all about the queer happenings to the tyre, as a new trouble presented itself. Dippy, making his usual change down to third, was greeted by a loud 'clonk' from somewhere underneath, and the engine screamed up; a chain had broken, and I looked round to see it writhing on the sand behind us. We hobbled round the bend in top gear and slowly gained speed down the straight, to the next bend, where Dippy intended to use second gear to get round. Another 'clonk' and second gear chain shot out behind to join the litter on the sand.

We were now left with only top gear, but we reckoned that there could not be many laps to go, and we were determined to finish if it was humanly possible. Dippy found that if he treated the course as a circle rather than an oval he would not reduce speed too much on the turns, although of course he would have a far greater distance to cover. To follow this course involved driving out to sea until we were almost dashing through the surf, and then coming inland until we were almost on the soft sand of the dunes.

After the second lap of these tactics we came out of the turn to see, far away down the straight, the finishing flag waving, and almost before we knew it we had passed the line and pulled into the paddock—the last of those who were classed as finishers. It mattered little to us that we were last; we had finished, and we had never enjoyed ourselves more.

Soaked with spray and caked with sand, we dismounted and looked over our little car, which we considered had stood up very well to the pounding. All seemed in order until we came to the offside rear tyre, and we were amazed to see that it was now completely devoid of rubber and had been running for some time on the bare canvas. A short examination was enough to show us the cause.

It appears that the spare wheel carried by us during the race was, quite unknown to us, an oversize by more than half an inch. When we had hastily fitted this wheel after our tyre had burst we had failed to notice that the tread of the larger tyre was in hard contact with a bracket used to support the unusual side-starting handle fitted to all G.N.s, and this bracket had steadily chewed into the rubber until there was nothing left but the canvas. The smell of rubber, which had first attracted my attention, had ceased when sufficient rubber had been removed to clear the bracket.

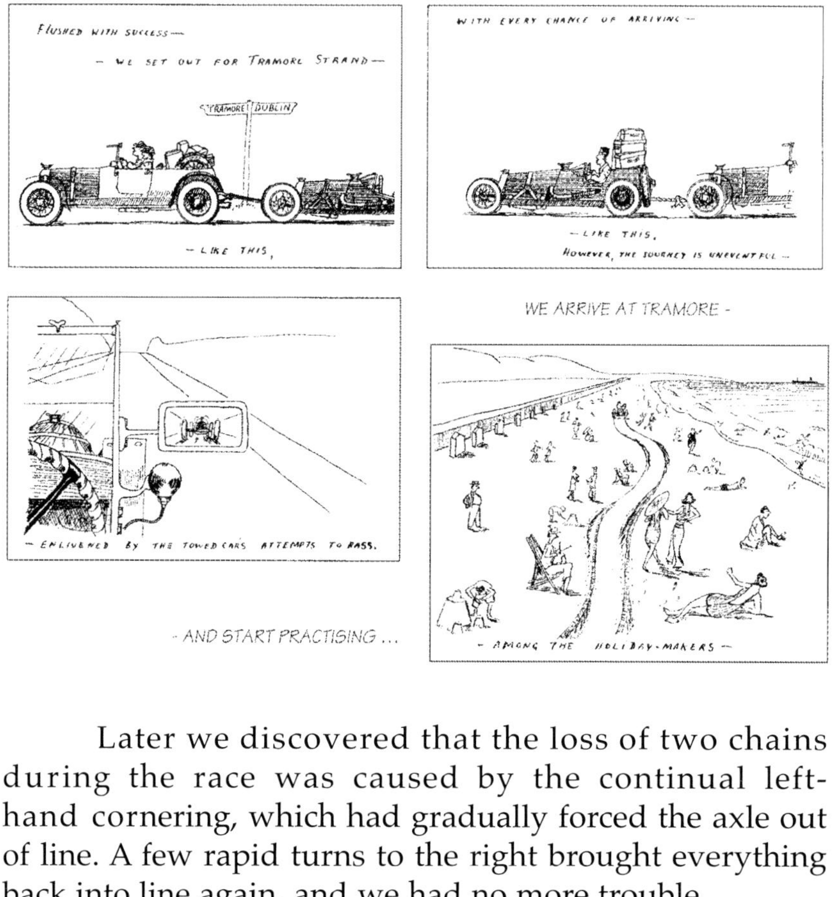

Later we discovered that the loss of two chains during the race was caused by the continual left-hand cornering, which had gradually forced the axle out of line. A few rapid turns to the right brought everything back into line again, and we had no more trouble.

Tramore races were over, and I think the adventure remains more vividly in my memory than any other motoring experience that has come my way, before or after.

That evening we attended the prize distribution in the dance hall in the centre of the town. There were no prizes for us, but our University Club was not without honour, as the motor-cycle race held in conjunction with the car event was won by that grand little sportsman, Gillie Campbell, who had ridden a magnificent race on his Levis machine.

We spent another uncomfortable but uneventful night in the open, and the next day we brought our strange outfit safely back to Dublin and home.

CHAPTER XV.
Craigantlet

SOME weeks after our inglorious efforts at Tramore, we decided that another event in distant parts would be very welcome, and our thoughts turned to the famous hill-climb held annually at Craigantlet, not far from the Ulster Tourist Trophy course. This climb was usually held on the week-end preceding the T.T. race.

We obtained and perused a copy of the regulations, and came to the conclusion that, while we would have little hope of winning any prizes as the events were mostly arranged in 'scratch' classes, we might not disgrace ourselves—and it would be very good fun.

Accordingly, the usual sketchy preparations were made, and in due course we set out for the North, Dippy's Riley towing the 'Horror' at the end of my automatic self-steering tow-bar.

We had a pleasant, uneventful trip on the wide road to Belfast, and we now had such faith in the tow-bar that only an occasional glance at the driving mirror was sufficient to assure us that the G.N. was still following obediently. All went well, and our first stop was at the customs post on the border between what was then the Irish Free State and Northern Ireland, where we had our first contretemps.

Now, in making preparations for this trip into Northern Ireland we had been careful to obtain a triptyque for the Riley, but it had not occurred to either of us that it would be necessary to do the same for the 'Horror'. Consequently we were somewhat put out when confronted by the customs officials, who informed us that we could go no further without the necessary papers. However, after some persuasion, they agreed to let us proceed if we filled in some forms and provided that we would deposit in cash one-third the value of the car. We carefully filled in all the required particulars, and in the space labelled 'Approximate Value of the Vehicle' we inscribed '£1-10-0' and handed the form to the officer in charge. He scrutinised the paper, and we watched his expression change from tolerance to antagonism.

"Now see here," he stormed, "we agreed to make a concession and let you through, but we're not here to be made fools of. What's the meaning of this nonsense?" jabbing the offending form with his thumb.

'But listen," said Dippy, "that's our true estimate of the value of the car. You haven't even seen it yet."

Grimly the excise man stumped out of his hut and stood in the road, staring at the odd equipage. Without a word, he turned on his heel, strode into the office, initialled the form, accepted our ten-shilling note, and issued a receipt. Then he sat back and fixed us with a baleful eye. "Will ye get to hell out of here," he exploded, "and take that yoke with you."

We lost no time in leaving the Border behind us, and an hour or so later we arrived at the foot of Craigantlet Hill, where competitors and the first of the large crowd of spectators were beginning to assemble in the glaring heat of the mid-day sun.

There was no proper paddock at Craigantlet, and the competing cars were lined up on the roadside while their owners fussed around them, making final adjustments. We parked the 'Horror' at the end of the line, and as there was plenty of time, we strolled up the road to see what was going on and to try to find out something about the system of starting and the type of corners on the hill. I had never seen the road before, and the only knowledge I had of it was obtained from the rough sketch supplied with the regulations for the hill-climb. I gathered that the course was about 1,000 yards long and that there were a few wide sweeping hairpin bends and some fast stretches near the finish.

While we were chatting with other drivers, I noticed that a small group of Important People with armlets bearing such titles as 'CHIEF MARSHAL' and 'CHIEF SCRUTINEER' were slowly coming down the line examining each car for possible faults and making notes on official-looking forms. As we watched them testing steering gear, shaking wheels and manipulating brakes, an uneasy feeling began to take hold of me, and this nervousness increased as they drew nearer the 'Horror'. I felt just like a candidate awaiting an oral examination.

At last the group of scrutineers reached our G.N., and we stood in the background covertly watching their expressions in an effort to gauge their reactions. Some looked faintly amused and others frankly incredulous. I must admit they had reason to raise their eyebrows, as the old car with its spindly wheels and amateurish bodywork looked definitely out of place in this concourse of sleek racers and up-to-date sports models.

The leader of the party warily approached the 'Horror' and shook one of the front wheels. The whole car shuddered and rattled. He then applied the hand-brake, while his assistant gave a light push behind. The car cheerfully moved up the road. There was a muttered conference and the scrutineering committee moved closer, while the leading spirit tried the steering wheel; they seemed quite surprised when the front wheels moved in rough relation to it. They pulled the wheel round to full lock, and then they all gathered round the front end, prodding and shaking. Another conference, with much solemn head-shaking, and then they approached us, the miserable owners.

They were very sorry—they knew we had come all the way from Dublin—very sporting and all that—but they had their duty with regard to the safety of the public.

No, they were very sorry; the car would not pass the scrutiny, and must be declared a non-starter.

Before the realisation of this blow had fully sunk in, I asked what particular points they were criticising. The spokesman said that there were a number of small discrepancies, but the chief thing that worried them was the fact that the tyres actually came in contact with the chassis when the steering was put to full lock, in either direction. This, he considered, was definitely unsafe, and was their main criticism.

The scrutineers then left us and went on their way down the road, leaving us in utter despondency sitting on the bank, thinking black thoughts about officials in general and scrutineers in particular.

As I sat there, miserably brooding on our misfortune and staring at the offending steering gear in front of me, I was suddenly struck by an idea. Surely, if this point about the tyres rubbing the chassis was the only thing worrying them, surely something could be done about it. There was still half an hour before the first event: could we not try something?

A little hard thought, and a rough calculation by eye— and the solution came to me. Still clamped to the front axle were the various lugs and fittings used for attaching my patent automatic tow-bar, which we had used to bring the car from Dublin. Now if these fittings were moved to the extremities of the axle, surely they could be arranged in such a way that they would limit the movement of the steering gear. Hastily we got to work, and in a very short time the job was complete and satisfactory in every way; the tyres were now quite incapable of touching the chassis, no matter what way the steering wheel was turned.

We decided that the next step was to make a formal appeal against the decision of the scrutineers, and to demand a new examination. With this resolve, we marched straight to the headquarters of the organisers, which was a small tent by the roadside, near the start, and were ushered into the presence of no less a personage than Colonel Lindsay Lloyd, the steward appointed by the Royal Automobile Club to preside over the event. The colonel listened to our appeal sympathetically, and in spite of the usual last-minute 'flap' before the start of an event, he managed to collect the scrutineering committee together and to bring them down the road to where the 'Horror' was parked. Another examination, in which the car was pummelled and its steering wheel twiddled. A short but deep conference, and then Mr. McLeod, the Chief Scrutineer, addressed us. They were still not altogether satisfied with the condition of the car, but taking into consideration our enthusiasm in coming all the way from Dublin to compete, they had decided to let us run in the event.

We were overcome with joy at the decision to allow us to run, and we immediately moved the car up into its allotted position among the waiting competitors, and in a few minutes we heard a crescendo of sound from an open exhaust as the first competitor to be sent off screamed his way up the twisty hill.

Car after car was given the signal and accelerated away, to disappear out of sight round the first bend, and almost before I realised it I was on the line.

The start at Craigantlet was conducted by an official who stood beside the competitor and clutched a telephone in his hand. He would shout the number of the car and the signal to start in such a way that it would be heard by the driver and also by the time-keepers, who were stationed at the finishing line. The time taken for the climb would then be telephoned back to the headquarters at the start, and announced for the benefit of the spectators through a system of loudspeakers.

It was my turn to have first run, and I sat at the wheel tense and keyed up with suppressed excitement and expectancy, first gear engaged and everything ready to make the best possible getaway.

"Number Seventeen—Three—Two—One—Go."

We shot off the line in great style. Full revs in first gear— a quick change into second, and foot hard down again. Brakes hard on for the first left-hand hairpin. Safely round with not much road to spare, and then a short straight to the next hairpin to the right. Another dab at the brake and we were round this with a protesting squeal from the tyres. Another steep, straight section, and then a difficult left-hand bend with high banks, crowded with spectators.

Swinging into this bend, I was about to take it at what I felt was the outside safety limit, when—Bang. The car lurched wildly, and a tearing, screeching sound came from underneath. The off front wheel had left its hub and was now wobbling and bouncing up the road ahead of me, while the car slid outwards and came to rest gently against the bank.

Now, it was by no means an unusual occurrence for the 'Horror' to shed a wheel, and, in fact, it had happened so often that we were quite used to the experience. I was therefore in no way put about on this occasion, but I must admit it was a little embarrassing in front of all those people.

Having retrieved the errant wheel from some distance up the road, I hastily refitted it, and in a very short time I was under way again, to complete my run up the hill. I heard afterwards that my time for the run was under six minutes, and as the average time for a car completing the course without incident was about 90 seconds, this allowed about four and a half minutes for the wheel-losing act.

In due course, when all the cars in the class had completed their runs, we were returned to the foot of the hill. I was glad to find that news of the lost wheel had not reached the scrutineers, so Dippy Harris took his place at the wheel for his run up the hill in the next class. He had an uneventful run and his time was 111 seconds, which was by no means a disgrace with the old car.

As it happened, the Craigantlet Hill-Climb of that year, 1933, was rather a dull event. No records had been broken and there were no serious accidents. The newspaper reporters were short of 'copy' and seized on the accident to the 'Horror' with delight. We were amazed when the Sunday papers reached us to be confronted with startling headlines, 'MOMENT OF TERROR'; 'RACING CAR LOSES WHEEL AT SIXTY MILES AN HOUR', and a lurid account of how I and hundreds of spectators had avoided death by inches. The winners of the events were hardly mentioned at all.

COMING DOWN

After the wheel-losing act at Craigantlet Hill Climb 'Dippy' Harris anxiously watches the offending wheel

CHAPTER XVI.

Road and Furrow

IT was not long after the Craigantlet adventure when my family suffered a sad loss which was to alter the course of my life.

My father, who had been in failing health for some time, was stricken by a partial paralysis, and after a short struggle had died peacefully. My mother was left with a large family and a 300-acre farm, mortgaged to the barn roofs, and suffering from under-stocking and under-cultivation.

At this time I was in the third year of the Engineering Course at Trinity College, and I was faced with the necessity of making a decision which would affect the future of myself and my family.

Should I endeavour to be an Engineer or a Farmer?

My academic career had not so far been what might be described as brilliant, and in fact I had grave doubts as to my ability to pass the final examinations for the Engineering Degree. Taking into account the meagre amount of study that I had found time for between rowing and 'special' building, it was likely that another long year would be necessary, even with a good deal of hard work. Even if I were successful, I had not made up my mind as to what branch of the profession I would support; there was no ready-made niche waiting for me, and there would probably be many years of apprenticeship to be undergone before I would become self-supporting. If I left home as a prospective engineer there would be nobody to carry on the farm, which would have to be sold, a new home found for my family, and the land of my fathers and forefathers would pass into strange hands.

On the other hand, if I decided to become a farmer I would do so at a time when farming was at its lowest ebb, I would be without capital, and I would be faced with years and years of scraping and financial uncertainty, living at the outside edge of a banker's benevolence. But I would have and hold the home and soil which my forbears had been proud to hand down from generation to generation.

I decided to try farming.

Having been brought up in farming surroundings, I was not entirely ignorant of agricultural matters, and it was soon clear to me that a certain degree of mechanisation was essential. It was in this field that my intimate associations with the Dublin scrap-yards became invaluable, and it was not long before I had found a tractor and other equipment for a very small outlay.

My mechanical knowledge and my experience in dealing with refractory motor cars was of great benefit, and I was able to put this very second-hand equipment in fair working order. I applied myself to the task of learning the art of ploughing and other tractor work, and of adjusting myself to the now habitual speed of three miles per hour. I also found that the smattering of civil engineering which I had picked up in college was to be very useful as I became involved in repairs to barns and bridges, and in the improvement of the farm drainage.

However, these writings are mainly of motoring and motor sport, and I have only referred to these changes in my way of life in so far as they affected my participation in these things.

It was at this time that there was another event which influenced my motoring activities. My college friend, 'Dippy' Harris, had qualified as a doctor and had left to take up the position of house-surgeon in a hospital in Derby. As a parting gift he left me his share in our racing G.N., so I now became sole owner of the 'Horror'. I decided to convert it into a sports car, which I could use for both reliability trials and speed events, and the next few months—in the off-time from farming were spent in dismantling and rebuilding to suit the new requirements.

SAINT PATRICK'S DAY TRIAL

Typical group at the start of a reliability Trial. 'Dippy' Harris's Anzani Nash, The Rover Nash and Paddy Le Fanu's Austin Swallow

Now, it is one thing to build a pure racing car, just an engine, chassis, and body shell, and quite another thing to construct a complete road car with all the necessary equipment. I had to have a full two-seater body, decently upholstered and fitted with windscreen and mudguards. There would also be a battery, self-starter, lights, horn, and hood to think about. There seemed to be endless planning and designing and altering, and countless visits to the scrap merchants for all the various parts required. At times I almost despaired of ever completing the job, but before the winter was fully over I was able to stand back and

The Rover Nash at the start line of Mount Venus Hill Climb 1934

admire my handiwork. I think it was quite a creditable effort—at least, so it seemed to me—and did not look out of place when seen in company with other sports cars. In appearance it resembled a cross between a Frazer Nash and the M.G. Midget, which was becoming popular at the time, and its performance was comparable with many light cars of the day. Its one weak point was the wheels; at the best of times they were nothing more than overgrown bicycle wheels, and now that the car was fully equipped, they looked altogether out of proportion. Not only had they this spindly appearance, but I had found no satisfactory method to secure them to the hubs, and they were liable to fly off at the most awkward moments. I am convinced that if I had been able to obtain a set of up-to-date centre-lock wheels and tyres I would have been the owner of a thoroughly satisfying little motor car.

When the rebuilding job was completed, I taxed the car and it became my means of personal transport for more than year. It was now graced by the more dignified title of Rover Nash, and it was to be seen in the paddock or car-park at all the race meetings and sprint events in the country. It was also driven in many reliability trials and collected some second-class awards.

CHAPTER XVII.

'Mick' Burke

IT was through the Rover Nash and its habit of shedding wheels at awkward moments that I was to meet a man who was to have a tremendous influence on my attitude towards the tuning and running of fast motor cars.

I was returning home one dark and wet night from a business trip to Dublin. The road was wet, visibility was at its worst, and I was travelling perhaps rather faster than I should under the circumstances. Suddenly I found myself confronted by the back of an enormous vehicle, which seemed to be stopped in the middle of the road, and which was entirely without lights. Instinctively I braked and swung the steering wheel wildly—quite the wrong thing to do, of course, but there was nothing else for it. I missed the obstruction, which turned out to be the trailer of a lorry which had come adrift, virtually by inches, and then became involved in a hair-raising skid on the wet road, which seemed to go on for ever. As we entered what seemed to me to be the third gyration, I felt the usual jar and tearing sound which signified that another wheel had parted company from its hub, and almost in the same second the car slid off the road. The naked hub dug into the ground and the whole car turned over on top of me.

I found myself completely unhurt, if a little dazed, more by the complete unexpectedness of the whole incident than through any shock. I crawled out from underneath and began to take stock of my surroundings. Somewhat to my surprise, I found that the final swerve of the car had taken it right between the petrol pumps of a roadside garage, and it was now resting neatly, although inverted, on the gravel patch between the pumps and the doors of the building.

It was only then that I realised that there was a silent, awestruck witness of the debacle. Standing in the shadow of the garage door, apparently struck speechless and immobile by my sudden inverted arrival, was the garage hand who happened to be on duty that evening. Until I wriggled out from under the wreckage, he was quite certain that not only had he a corpse on his hands, but also the likelihood of a conflagration among his petrol pumps. Imagine, then, his relief when I used a few well-chosen expletives to express my feelings at having wrecked my little car. In later years I have heard Mick Burke (for that was the name of my silent witness) recount this story and describe how unmoved I was by the affair. In fact, he said that he got the impression that that was the way I always pulled up for petrol, and that he would not have been surprised if I had casually remarked: "Fill her up, and check the tyres." Little did he realise that I was far too overcome to act otherwise.

When we had recovered our senses we dragged the car inside the garage and surveyed the damage, and it was soon obvious that a considerable amount of work would have to be done before it would be in a condition to run again. I told him that I was not in a position to pay a large garage bill for repairs, and it then came out that he had been longing to get his hands on just such a car as this for years, and he offered to help me with it in his spare time. I was glad to accept the offer, and in this way it came about that we spent many pleasant evenings, working and chatting, and discussing the latest developments in all types of motor sport.

Mick Burke was a man in his early forties and somewhat above the usual garage mechanic type. During my association with him I learnt a good deal of his early history, and gathered that he had been something of a firebrand in his youth. He had become involved in the strife of the 'troubled times' in Ireland. He now carried his left leg stiff from the hip as a result of a bullet in some escapade, and was prematurely grey from the terrors and privations suffered while among the boys who 'took to the hills'. All these were things of the past, and he now had a fine contempt for anything to do with politics.

I soon realised that here was a mechanic of exceptional ability, to whom time and trouble meant nothing when the machine under his care was anything in the nature of a sports car. I began to recommend him to any of my friends who might want work done on their cars, and shortly after our first meeting he gave up his job at the roadside garage and started to work for himself in a tiny shed behind his house in the suburbs of Dublin. At almost any time the tail of a sports car could be seen sticking out from this shed, while streams of, to say the least, forceful language would issue from the doors as he struggled with some inaccessible portion.

But to return to my Rover Nash and the work of repairing it. It did not take Mick Burke long to discover several weak points in the design, and he was frankly horrified at the lack of such safety devices as split pins and lock washers. I'm afraid to say I made light of his grim warnings, and we proceeded with the work on the car, which became more or less roadworthy again in a couple of weeks. I drove it away one evening, with much head-shaking and many disparaging remarks from Mick, and not many days later I was to learn to take him more seriously.

I was driving the car along a straight portion of the main road near my home. The speed was about 50 m.p.h. and I was thinking of nothing in particular when it suddenly dawned on me that the steering wheel in my hands was not attached to anything. A quick look down confirmed this, and there lying on my lap was the bolt which was supposed to be holding the wheel on its column. There was no time to think, and little time to act.

Carefully I pushed the wheel back on to the protruding stump of shaft, and with my left hand picked up the fallen bolt and gently eased it back into its hole. Fortunately the road was smooth, wide and straight at this point, and more fortunately still, there was no other traffic. The car maintained an approximately straight line during this operation, and I was able to bring it to a gentle standstill without mishap, but with a distinct feeling of 'butterflies in the stomach'.

Not long after this narrow escape I was driving through the village of Clondalkin at moderate speed, and while making a sharp right turn there was a click from somewhere underneath, and the steering wheel spun round ineffectively in my hands. The car described a wide arc, mounted the pavement, and went straight into the sombre gate of the police station. A brief examination showed that the steering arm—a drop-forging which I had heated and bent to suit my purpose—had chosen this moment to break clean across. Little damage was done, but when I think of what might have happened, I shudder.

Needless to say, when Mick Burke came to hear of these things his remarks became even more disparaging, and the air was full of "I-told-you-so's". I began to take his advice more seriously, and ceased to scorn the use of split-pins—at least, in the steering gear and braking system.

CHAPTER XVIII.
The 'Ulster'

AT about the time that my friend and mentor, Mick Burke, had succeeded in convincing me that my home-made car was not a suitable vehicle for ordinary use on the public roads, a little car was offered for sale in Dublin, and within reasonable limits with regard to price. This was a car for which I had suffered a secret longing for many years, and was, in fact, one of the famous 'Ulster' Austin Sevens. I well remember the impression these great little cars had made in the Tourist Trophy races of the early thirties, when the bright orange painted 'works teams' had buzzed round among the thundering Bentleys and Alfa Romeos, like so many lady-birds. Never had I dreamt that one might come within my reach, so when I heard of one advertised for less than £40 I lost no time in finding the owner and getting him to promise to hold it until I could raise the money.

I found the owner—in hospital. He had bought the little Austin with a view to taking up motor racing. His fond mother, who had a horror of racing cars, had promised him that if he would only give up this mad idea, she would buy him a horse, and he could take up hunting. He had given in to his mother's wish; the horse was duly presented, he had gone out hunting—and had broken his neck. He was now due for a sojourn of many months in hospital, and the car was for sale—cheap. Also the horse, I assume.

The next step was to find the purchase price. My old Austin Seven, which had served me so well, had long since been relegated to the position of farm hack, and was thoroughly dilapidated and rapidly falling to pieces. However, two hard days of patching, painting, and tuning of the 'sawdust-in-the-back-axle' variety made it look fairly passable. Another two days of high pressure salesmanship, and I had succeeded in getting enough for it to cover a down-payment on the coveted Ulster Model. In another day the car was my property, and safely installed in Mick Burke's diminutive workshop.

I was now the proud possessor of what was to all intents and purposes a thoroughbred racing car, and I found myself walking round in a sort of glowing daze. Never had I dreamt that such a thing would come my way.

As there are very few of these amazing little machines on the road to-day, perhaps a description would not be out of place. Basically it was the same as the ordinary touring Austin Seven, but the chassis had been cunningly lowered, and the springing stiffened considerably. The engine was also based on the touring unit, but had a much heavier crankshaft and other refinements, such as a water pump and aluminium cylinder head. On the left side was mounted a large Cozette supercharger tucked under the beautifully shaped exhaust pipes, which swept out through a slot in the bonnet and led to a large plated silencer and racy looking tail pipe. The body was a very light two-seater, devoid of such luxuries as doors, and shaped to a short pointed tail, which housed the spare wheel. The road wheels were partly covered by skimpy little mudguards.

As regards performance, the makers claimed about 75m.p.h. for the ordinary model as sold across the counter, but one had covered a mile at 94 m.p.h. on the sand in 1931 My particular model never bettered about 70 m.p.h., but it was in the lower gears that it really showed its form. It would do almost 60 m.p.h. in second gear, and the acceleration was something to marvel at. The steering and road holding took a lot of getting used to, and the brakes were a very weak point, although they responded well to careful adjustment.

No sooner had Mick Burke got his hands on my new possession than he insisted that it should be completely dismantled and should have a thorough overhaul. I meekly submitted, and there followed many evenings of absorbing and highly instructive work. I was to learn how a good mechanic sets about the task of preparing a car to his own satisfaction, while I tried to curb my impatience and the desire to get motoring. It was an eye-opener to me to see how much trouble could be taken over the fitting of bearings and the grinding of valves. Doubtful ball races, that would have passed my rather slap-dash examination, were discarded, slightly stretched bolts or burred nuts were replaced, and everything was cleaned and polished like the works of a watch. Split-pins and other locking devices were meticulously used in every conceivable place. In the meantime I busied myself with the work on the somewhat dilapidated bodywork. I hammered out the dents, scraped it all down, and carefully applied a coat of paint in a shade as near as I could get to 'Bugatti blue'. I employed a local upholsterer to do what he could with the rather tattered seats, and the final result was really quite pleasing to the eye.

The supercharged 1936 'Ulster' Austin

Eventually, and far sooner than I had hoped, the great day for the first test run arrived. I was thrilled with the whine of the supercharger, and the apparent eagerness of the little car to get going. I left the shed with many grim warnings from Mick Burke to keep the revs down and to give the engine a chance during the running-in process. During the next couple of hundred miles I got to know and love the willing little machine.

At about this time the annual hill-climb at Kilternan, the event which I like to think of as that which I helped to inaugurate, was about to be run by the University Club. I entered my Austin, and began to make the necessary preparations.

Now, there is one unsatisfactory matter in the organisation of hill-climbs in Ireland, and that is the difficulty of arranging for practice on the chosen hill. It is difficult enough to obtain permission to use the road for the event itself, without arranging for the road to be closed for a preliminary period. The result is that competitors must either attempt to practise unofficially while the road is open to the ordinary public, or they must do without any practice at all. The former is extremely dangerous, both to competitors and the unsuspecting public; the latter is also uncomfortable and dangerous. A driver cannot be expected to show his best form when he has had no opportunity to study the course.

What usually happened was that a sort of unofficial, but controlled, practice was arranged among competitors on the evening before, and on the morning, of the event. Competitors would assemble at the bottom of the hill, and scouts would be placed at suitable vantage points. When the road was deemed to be clear the scouts would make a pre-arranged signal, and the competitors would have a go,

The Supercharged 'Ulster' Austin competing in a flying half-mile 'sprint', in a sylvan setting at Turvey Avenue, Donabate.

one at a time. When they had all reached the top they would turn and come down together for another run. Just such an arrangement was made on the morning of this particular event, and I duly turned up with my Ulster Austin.

This organisation of unofficial practising worked very well as a rule, but it depended very much on the alertness and efficiency of the scouts placed at the blind corners. These helpers had no authority, and were not provided with flags. It could happen, therefore, that if any ordinary motorist, or competitor, for that matter, chose to disregard or misunderstand these signals there might be an accident, or what Sammy Davis calls a 'phenomenal avoidance'.

It so happened on this occasion that one competitor, driving a very fast Alfa Romeo, had chosen to visit the hill by an unusual route, and arrived at the top of the hill instead of the bottom where competitors were awaiting their turns for a run. This driver was unaware that practice was in progress, and proceeded down the hill. He mistook the frantic wavings of the scouts for the friendly greetings of fellow-enthusiasts, and went on his way—just at the time I was due for my practice run. I was nicely placed on the wrong side of the road, and about to take a sharp right-hand corner, and I must admit that I also failed to notice the signals of the agitated watchers. At this point I found myself confronted by a hard-looking Alfa radiator—and I immediately proceeded to take avoiding action. I swerved violently to the left, and the little car responded, but the near-side wheels rose high in the air. I felt myself falling from the car, and threw out my left hand to grab any support to hold myself in. We proceeded some 30 yards up the road in this manner, two wheels high in the air, while a searing pain in my left hand told me that I was holding on to the exhaust pipe. I let go with a yell, and at the same time the Austin bumped into the stone wall at the edge of the road, and came to a sudden stop.

Ruefully I got out and examined the car for damage while I nursed my blistered hand. To my amazement there seemed to be no serious damage other than a badly buckled front wheel. Not serious, except for the fact that I had no spare.

We dragged the car off the road, and I walked down the hill disconsolately, while the practice runs continued. In the improvised paddock I met Mick Burke, and told him that I was out of the event for want of a wheel. He looked at his watch. Twelve-thirty on a Saturday morning If he hurried, he could just make it. He jumped into his old Morris, and set out to drive furiously the ten odd miles back into Dublin against the traffic, to catch the Austin agents before they closed for the week-end. In the meantime I was seized by the ambulance men who had arrived by this time to take up duty for the event. They set about making a good job of my burnt hand, obviously delighted at having a customer so early in the proceedings.

In due course Mick Burke arrived back, armed with a brand new wheel and the necessary tools to change over the tyre; and in a very short time the Austin was on its wheels again and back in the paddock, awaiting its turn for the official attack on the hill.

As to the actual event, I cannot say much about my performance. The Austin acquitted itself well, but not well enough to figure in the lists of awards. It happened that there was another Ulster Austin competing, and this car was the property of a man who had all the resources of a big machine shop behind him. It was just that much faster than mine. and won all the awards in our class. Or perhaps it was driven that much better.

The career of my beloved 'blown' Austin was short, if not without incident. I drove it in one or two more speed events, with no marked success, and then continued to use it in the winter for touring. One week-end in early December I was asked by friends in the south of Ireland to join a shooting party, and I duly set out in the Austin on a bitterly cold afternoon, armed with suitcase and gun. The car seemed to be running extra sweetly in the frosty air, and I was enjoying the longish run. I was driving on one of the long, straight roads which abound in the midlands of this country, and was gradually turning up the wick until the speed was in the neighbourhood of 65 miles an hour. All seemed to be going smoothly when suddenly, and completely without warning, there was a sickening bang and scrunch from the engine compartment—and the engine stopped dead from almost its maximum. Not only did the engine stop, but the back wheels were locked, and the car was screeching along sliding all over the road. I pressed the clutch, but with no result. I wrestled with the gear lever, but it would not come out of gear. Gradually the car slewed to a halt, smoke rising from the two rear tyres, while a widening pool of oil and water spread out on the road from under the engine. I climbed out and surveyed the car, hardly daring to lift the bonnet. When I eventually nerved myself to do so, I was greeted with such a scene of devastation as I have never seen under one bonnet, before or since.

There was literally nothing left whole in the space where the neat little engine had been. All I could see was a jumble of pieces of aluminium and cast iron. Twisted connecting rods stuck out at grotesque angles, and the hooped camshaft seemed to be wound round what was left of the shattered crankshaft. Here, indeed, was an engine which could be deemed 'completely written off'.

I will never forget the misery of the long, weary bus trip back to Dublin. On the following day Mick Burke offered to help me to get the remains of the Austin home, and we set off in an old Ford van borrowed for the occasion. Mick insisted on sitting in the Austin for the long tow home, and he now claims that a hundred miles on tow in an open two-seater in the middle of winter is quite the coldest experience he has ever undergone.

The fate of the Austin had now to be decided. There was nothing for it but to do a 'patch-up' job and to get rid of it as soon as possible. I visited my favourite scrap yard, and after the usual bargaining I obtained an ordinary touring engine of about 1925 vintage for the sum of £2. We fitted this engine in place of the beautiful little supercharged unit, and after a certain amount of tuning, it ran tolerably well. I advertised the car, and the very first applicant immediately fell in love with it. He was not worried by the low performance of the engine—it was the appearance that took his fancy. In a very short time the deal was made and the car left my yard, leaving me with the price for which I had originally acquired it.

I never saw the little car again, but I was able to follow its; career through the advertisement columns of the daily papers, which made very instructive reading. It appears that it did not take the new owner long to realise that looks are not everything, and an advertisement appeared stating that a 'Racing Austin, perfect mechanical order, newly painted in blue, price £60' was on offer. The sale apparently went through, and a few weeks later there was another advertisement, obviously applying to the same car—this time a 'Super Sports Racing Austin, perfect, etc., price £80'. And so on, each new owner quickly realising that he had been 'sold a dud' and adding a little more to the qualifications and the demanded price.

No, I never saw the Austin again, but I am still reminded of those days by the presence in my workshop of bits of twisted metal which had once been the beautifully machined parts of a first-class racing engine.

CHAPTER XIX.
Back to Chains Again

AFTER the disposal of my supercharged Austin I found myself without a car, and such motoring as I was able to manage took place in the farm milk van, in the interval between milk rounds. I found this carless condition very dispiriting, as a sports car of some kind had become part of my very existence. I began to take steps to rectify this matter and kept my eyes and ears open for any news of a suitable vehicle which might be on the market.

It was during this interim period that I happened to meet a young man whose name will be well known to anyone who has followed motor-cycle racing. Manliff Barrington, for that is who it was, had reached the headlines in motor-cycle racing, and was well known in the Isle of Man and abroad. He had also turned his hand to car racing, and had soon proved that he was a 'natural' driver. He had been lucky enough to be offered a Frazer Nash to drive in the Leinster Trophy of 1936, and had finished third in that race. Needless to say, I had been an enthusiastic spectator of that event. At the time, I had thought to myself that of all the cars I had ever seen that Frazer Nash was the most desirable; so when he now mentioned that the owner was thinking of selling, all sorts of wild thoughts began to go through my mind. I knew very well that the price of this car would probably run into many hundreds of pounds, and that I might as well try to buy one of the T.T. Bentleys or Alfa Romeos; but when Barrington said that at any rate there was nothing to lose by approaching the owner, I fell in with the idea. When he offered to take me in the car as a trial run, the matter was clinched.

The owner of the Nash lived in a country town in Kildare, and we set out on the 40-mile run one crisp, bright day in early March. The car surged along in Manliff's expert hands in a manner quite different from anything to which I was accustomed, and before we had covered half the distance I had vowed to myself that some day, somehow, that Frazer Nash would be mine.

After an all-too-short and exhilarating run, we reached our destination, and I was being introduced, somewhat diffidently, to the owner of the wonderful car. Ainsley Verschoyle was a sportsman of the old school. Here was a well-built man in the late sixties, dressed in sporting tweeds and surrounded by guns and fishing rods. On the walls of his charming country house were many trophies of the chase, and at his heel one of the pointers for which he had become well known at field trials all over Ireland. In fact, a typical country gentleman.

Mr. Verschoyle had always had an interest in fast motor cars, and somewhat late in life he had decided to try his hand at motor racing. To this end he had ordered what he considered to be the ideal car for his purpose—a car which could be used for fast touring, and yet, without much special tuning, would be ready to enter in road races

Manliff Barrington racing the Frazer Nash in the 1936 Limerick Grand Prix

of the type popular in Ireland at the time. In fact, the current model of the famous Frazer Nash.

Unfortunately, the car had proved rather a handful for a man of his years, and after one race in the Phoenix Park in which he finished 11th at the very creditable speed of 70 m.p.h., he decided to relinquish the wheel to a younger man. The lucky driver of his choice was Desmond 'Gobbo' McCracken, who justified his selection by winning the Bray 'round-the-houses' in the following year. Later he had offered the car to Manliff Barrington who drove it successfully in several races, culminating in the third place in the Leinster Trophy race, already mentioned. He had now grown tired of seeing other people driving his car, being a man of action himself, and had decided that it was time to dispose of it and to buy something a little lighter in the controls.

When the time came to state the reason for our visit, I found myself tongue-tied. I was suddenly overcome by shame and embarrassment when I realised my utter cheek in even contemplating the purchase of such a car. After all, the price asked was approximately ten times what I had to offer. And then words came in a rush, and I told him frankly that I coveted his car; that I couldn't eat or sleep till I got it; that I would do anything short of murder to get it. If only he would make a special price I would be his slave for life. I did everything but get down on my knees and beg. In the end, and before I realised what I had done, Mr. Verschoyle had lowered his price to approximately half the original figure—and I had accepted.

I left in a sort of dream. My mind refused to register what I had done, and all I knew was that the Frazer Nash was mine. However, by the time we neared Dublin the practical side of the business began to impress itself on me, and I began to realise that somehow I had got to find the money. As soon as we reached the city I had a bright idea, and I went off to interview one of the large hire-purchase concerns. They listened sympathetically, but they were sorry, they didn't do business on second-hand cars, and in any case they couldn't undertake hire-purchase on a deal between private individuals. I tried another firm, and here I was in luck. The executive who interviewed me was interested in fast cars, and I managed to gain his sympathy. They didn't do business with second-hand cars either, but in this case they might make an exception. Finally, after an hour's argument and much form-filling, I left the office; and the Frazer Nash was as near to being mine as no matter, and two long years in which to pay for it.

Fay Taylour descending Craigantlet Hill Climb in 1936

Here was a car at last—a real car. Every inch of it seemed to have been designed with the express intention of exciting the covetous desires in a young man in his twenties. It simply bristled with fittings and extras which delight the heart of the enthusiast. It had a close-fitting two-seater body, with the characteristic 'bath-tub' tail, and a large petrol tank with enormous quick-action filler cap.

Graceful exhaust pipes swept out from the long bonnet and merged into a totally inadequate silencer. The gear lever and large hand brake were placed outside the body, for all to see, and it was fitted with twin aero screens and a large strap round the bonnet. The whole car was finished in a shade of brown most unusual in a sports car, which helped to make it even more remarkable. When I got it home and had more time to examine its more intimate details, I found that it was fitted with the well-tried Meadows 12 h.p. engine, with two beautiful carburettors. The back end contained a mass of chains, and close inspection showed me that it was almost identical with the old G.N., with which I was so familiar.

To drive this car was a revelation to me. There was a feeling of tremendous power, and yet the engine never seemed to be working hard. The springing was somewhat hard, but the car held the road like a leech. Cornering required quite a different technique to the ordinary car, as the lack of differential gear was inclined to make the tail swing out. This was rather disconcerting at first, but when one became used to it there seemed to be no better way of negotiating bends. The steering was extremely heavy, so much so that Barrington had had the wheel corded so that he could maintain a better hold. The clutch was also of the 'brute force' variety, and I could now understand why Mr. Verschoyle had relinquished the wheel to younger men. The brakes were excellent, but again a powerful right foot was necessary to obtain full effect.

Such was the car that I had virtually sold my soul to possess, and as I lovingly polished and cleaned it I swore that I would never misuse it or subject it to such things as competitions. I would never risk straining the engine in hill-climbs, and never, never would it be used for such rough sport as reliability trials. It was a car to be loved and cherished, and would do very nicely for transporting me in and out of the city, and occasional tours in the country.

Track and Field events

But such high-flown resolutions, made in the enthusiasm of early acquisition, are only made to be broken.

CHAPTER XX.
Phoenix Park

ONE day in the late summer of 1937 my post brought me a large envelope which contained the Supplementary Regulations and Entry Form for the International Grand Prix Race Meeting to be run by the Irish Motor Racing Club in the Phoenix Park.

As I read through this ponderous document a tiny thought began to ferment in my mind, and forced itself forward till it could not be disregarded. Why not, the thought kept repeating, have a go at the Phoenix Park race? I have a car just made for this type of race, and after all, what is the use of having a sports car if I don't use it for sport?

The idea grew and grew, and my eyes wandered to the paragraph about entry fees. Then I hastily pushed the papers into the back of a drawer. It said: "Entry fee £10 per person per car".

But the notion persisted, and I soon found myself perusing the regulations again. If only I had the entry fee, I do believe I would have a go.

Then I had another idea. The prize for first place in this race was fifty pounds. Surely there must be someone with some spare cash who might take a gamble, if I offered any prize money won against the entry fee. I developed this theme in my mind, and suddenly it came to me that I knew a possible victim.

On the outskirts of Dublin there lived a distant cousin, a lady who took an almost fanatical interest in motor racing. I had seen her ample figure at every race and speed event in the last five years. Even by dawn's early light, at the morning practices for the Phoenix Park races, I had seen her around the pit area, taking the keenest interest in everything that was going on, and she could talk for hours on anything connected with motor racing.

Now it occurred to me that this lady might be charmed at the idea of seeing motor racing 'from the inside'. If she would put up the paltry few pounds, she could enter my car for the race, and thereby occupy my pit and wear a brassard, in the proud capacity of 'Entrant'. In return she could have any prize money which I might win.

Once the idea had formed there was no going back, and eventually I took my courage in both hands and set out for the suburban residence of Phyllis Godfrey, for that was the name of my proposed benefactress. She listened to my plan sympathetically and eventually surrendered to my impassioned plea. I left with a heart full of gratitude, and clutching a cheque for no less than fifteen pounds.

……………………..

Having completed the formality of entering for the race (Phyllis Godfrey having flatly refused to allow her name to go forward as entrant), the next important step was the preparation of the car. Again I was handicapped by lack of funds, and I naturally decided to turn the full force of my diplomacy on to my friend and helpmate, Mick Burke. At this time Mick had gone into business on his own, and had set himself up in a small garage on the main road near my home.

I approached him and told him about the race. I then said that if he would help to prepare the car I would nominate him as reserve driver, and he would at least have the fun of a few practice laps before the event. Mick was delighted, and accepted with alacrity. In fact, I found myself immediately deprived of my car, as then and there he seized on it and started to pull it apart.

There followed many days and nights of intensive work, as Mick insisted on taking the car down to the last nut and bolt. Every part was cleaned and checked and reassembled with infinite care, and the entire resources of the little garage were given over to the preparation of the car. If any unfortunate private customer brought his family saloon along for greasing and oiling, he was looked on with such loathing that he would say that perhaps he would come back later, and then hastily withdrew.

Finally, and just before the day scheduled for the first practice, the job was completed to Mick's satisfaction, and we took out the Nash for a test run. I was astounded at the difference in the performance of the car. It had been transformed from a snappy sports car into a snarling, road-eating racer that seemed to be straining to get going. We took the car to a comparatively clear stretch of main road, and there we carried out carburettor and ignition tests, and when we finally called it a day we were satisfied that the speedometer needle would hover round the 90 mark for as long as the road remained straight and clear.

On the next evening we presented the Frazer Nash for official scrutiny, and we watched in some trepidation while Sam Robinson went over the car, examining everything minutely. Would he notice that one of the steering wheel spokes was slightly loose, or the tiny drip of oil from the sump? Would the race numbers which I had painted so painstakingly on the sides pass muster? No, everything was all in order, except one point. There must be a second return spring on the throttle control. He would examine the car in the morning, and if the spring was satisfactory we could consider that we had passed.

With lots of mumblings about a lot of silly nonsense, we took the car home, and having found a suitable spring, we fitted it and left everything ready in anticipation for the early morning start.

We were astir long before daylight, and we reached the pit area on the Phoenix Park course as the grey light of dawn was widening over the green expanse. Here was a scene of great activity as competitors and their cars began to arrive from all directions, and marshals hurried off to take up their appointed positions.

There was a peculiar and indefinable atmosphere about these early morning practice periods. The unwonted activity at such an hour, and the chill, rather eerie light; the feeling that this great public park had been taken over temporarily by a band of true enthusiasts—for only such would rise from their beds at 5 a.m.; the air of anticipation and suppressed excitement, apparent among drivers and officials alike; the numbers of unshaven chins among the normally spruce party of senior stewards; all these things, and many others, contributed to make these events quite different to anything else.

Presently, as the first rays of the morning sun began to disperse the light mist, we were given the signal to commence practising, and I pulled out from the pit area and set out for a couple of laps to warm up the oil and to get the feel of the course. Then back to my pit where Mick Burke and Phyllis Godfrey were fussing like a couple of hens whose chickens had gone out on the road, to report that all was well, except for a certain amount of wheel patter under heavy braking. A little adjustment to the shock absorbers, and I set off again, to put in three or four laps, almost as hard as I could go, while I endeavoured to note cut-off points and proper lines on the corners. I had plenty to learn, not the least being to remember that the continental pass-on-the-left rule of the road applied. After covering a few laps, and just as I was beginning to enjoy myself, I realised that time was getting on, and I pulled into the pits to let Mick have his turn at the wheel. He seemed only to have done two or three laps when the flag went up to signify the end of the practice period, and he returned to the pits, pronouncing himself well satisfied with the car. Before we left the Park we were informed that we had both qualified and were now entitled to compete in the race.

There was another practice period on the following morning, and we turned out again, to spend the valuable time in adjustments to shock absorbers and tyre pressures. We were satisfied that the engine was as right as we could make it, and was in no need of attention.

Close company with N.G. Wilson's MG K3 in the 'Park.

Then came the big day. September 11, 1937, and my first road race. We were among the first to arrive in the paddock, and as the crowds began to pour into the Park the minutes slowly ticked by. Although I think I remained outwardly fairly calm, I was suffering from a fair share of pre-race tension. Even the most hardened racing drivers suffer this affliction, so perhaps it was not unexpected on the occasion of my first big road race. The outward signs are the endless polishing of an already spotless vizor, and the zipping and unzipping of the leather jacket. More important things, such as the checking of plug lead terminals and the arrangement of the pit were forgotten. However, Miss Godfrey and Mick Burke soon had this matter in hand, and the pit counter was neatly arrayed with tools of every kind, spare chains, oil, water, and spare wheel ready to hand. We had arranged a large lap-sheet, and we also had a large signal board with which it was hoped to convey to me information as to how things were going during the race.

The race was to be a handicap event over 24 laps of the course, which was just under five miles round. Entries ranged from 'Bira' and Raymond Mays in two of the fastest cars of the time, to sundry Rileys and converted Fords, about 30 in all. My Frazer Nash was placed about half-way down the handicap, and was to get six credit laps. I would therefore only have to cover about 90 miles, and of course it would not be necessary to refuel.

As zero hour approached, the competing cars were wheeled out on to the starting grid, and were placed in four handicap groups, to be sent off at half-minute intervals. I found myself in company with six other cars which would leave the line together. Tensely we sat in our cars, throttles blipping, as we watched the starter and his assistant take up position, and wondered if that flag would ever drop. This is, perhaps, the worst few moments in racing. The flag was raised, and the air was filled with a crescendo of sound, deadening the ears and making it impossible to hear one's own engine. The flag swept down, and the seven cars surged forward in a mass, and slowly sorted themselves out into a straggling line. Thus we roared up the mile of straight, and then the warning boards for the famous Mountjoy corner appeared. This was a full right-angled turn, and necessitated braking from about 90 m.p.h. down to the speed at which it could be taken—about 35 m.p.h. in my case. I had selected a braking point near the second warning board, and I now braked heavily, with a protesting howl from the tyres, down into second gear, nicely round the corner which was taken gently on this first lap, and then down with the accelerator for a fast getaway. But . . . Nothing happened. There was no response to the throttle, and the car drifted along, to come to rest at the roadside, while my rivals flashed by.

For a short time I sat in the car, too stupefied to move. My brain just refused to register, in this sudden cessation of forward movement. The engine was still ticking over, but there was absolutely no response to my frantic jabbing at the pedal.

Then my numbed mind began to act again, and I jumped out and wrenched open the bonnet. There was the cause in front of my eyes. A nut had unscrewed itself and the throttle had become disconnected from the pedal. The spring which the scrutineers had insisted on being fitted had closed the throttle, and that was that.

In mental anguish I turned to the group of marshals which had collected round the car.

"For the love of Mike," I shouted, "has anyone got a quarter-inch B.S.F. nut?"

One of the marshals, who had a motor-cycle parked nearby, ran to his machine, opened his tool-box, and in an amazingly short time produced the required nut and a suitable spanner. It was the work of a few seconds to replace the nut and to tighten it, slam down the bonnet, jump in and then to tear away down the road in pursuit of the field. As I drove I fumed and cursed my luck. Surely this must have been the only nut in the whole car that Mick had not locked and pinned in position. I had lost fully three minutes, enough to destroy any hope of finishing in a high position. I drove on blindly, and soon I had lost all idea of the number of laps covered. As I passed the pits I caught a glimpse of Mick's harassed face, and tried to signify by gestures what had happened, but of course it was quite impossible to convey any meaning. I also saw my signal board thrust out from my pit as I passed, but in my agitation I completely forgot the meaning of the code we had arranged, so the signals meant nothing to me.

I settled down to drive steadily in the hope of finishing inside the time limit, and was beginning to enjoy myself hugely. What did it matter if I was unplaced—I had never expected to do any good, anyway. Here I was, driving in company with such famous names as Bira, Mays, and Whitehead; if I finished at all I could consider that I had done well. Incidentally, 'driving in company' is a more apt expression than may be realised, for I saw more of Prince Bira and his Maserati than anyone else in that race. Bira was lapping at about 105 m.p.h., and, owing to my position in the handicap, it was necessary for him to pass me more than six times in order to lead me in the race. Being passed by the Maserati was one of the most shattering experiences I had undergone. It would roar past unexpectedly, with about 40 miles per hour to spare, and for a couple of seconds I would receive the exhaust full in my face. Then it would recede in the distance, and in what seemed be about five minutes there it would be, roaring past again, having lapped me in the interval. This would happen regularly throughout the race.

After we had been motoring steadily for what seemed a short time I was taken completely by surprise on approaching the pit area to see the chequered flag waving to signify the end of the race. I just couldn't believe that it was over so soon.

One more lap at reduced speed and I pulled into the paddock amidst the hubbub always found there at the end of a race. I was immediately approached by Mick Burke, who was bursting to know what had happened on that first lap. When I told him, his face was contorted by an expression of disgust which did not wear off for many months. I think he would have kicked himself then and there if it hadn't been for his stiff leg. He has never ceased to blame himself for that one lapse.

Phyllis Godfrey took the whole thing very philosophically, like the true sportsman she was. I don't think she ever expected or hoped to get any return for her money, and I think she enjoyed taking part in the pitwork.

The Frazer Nash had performed magnificently, and had never faltered except on that first lap. I was credited with eighth place, at an average speed of almost 74, and in due course I received a little silver plaque from the Irish Motor Racing Club as a reminder of this, my first road race.

CHAPTER XXI.
The Veterans

EARLY in I938 energetic committee members of the Leinster Motor Club had the idea that a competition for veteran cars, on the lines of the famous London Brighton run, might go down well in Ireland. All members of the motoring fraternity were notified and there was an immediate and favourable response, not only from the sporting element, but also from among those who had treasured the old cars which had been carefully stored away (and forgotten) since the days of our fathers.

The Leinster Club realised that it was unlikely that there were sufficient really old cars in the country, and it was decided that there should be some latitude in the age of the contestants. Eventually it was decided that any car built before the 1914 war should be eligible, and there would be age groups for the cars of various periods.

The date for the event was finally fixed for a Saturday at the end of June, and the whole idea caught on like wildfire among the motoring enthusiasts. There was a frantic search for old cars in a fit condition to run.

The venture was just the kind of thing that appealed to me and I began to cast round for a suitable vehicle. I bemoaned what seemed to me the improvidence of my father in disposing of the beautiful old cars in which I remembered many journeys as a boy; but how was he to know that one day they might be period pieces?

Actually I had not far to look. Less than a mile away, parked in an old barn, was a little car which had once been the means of locomotion of a venerable dignitary of the Church. lt had passed into the possession of an elderly lady who had now reached the age when motoring in a very exposed vehicle had lost its charm, and so it had been relegated to the corner of a shed where it had stood in lonely dignity for many years, gathering dust and cobwebs.

A little diplomacy over a cup of afternoon tea was all that was necessary to extract a loan of the car for this event, and with many promises that it would be returned in better condition than ever before, I joyfully went out to the shed to dig out my latest competition machine.

The 1911 Renault is unearthed

The car was a Renault of about 1911, in very good condition and complete in every detail. The two-cylinder engine reposed in a sort of box at the front, and the body consisted of two very high seats and a folding 'dicky' behind. It had a folding hood which would have looked well on a horse brougham. The dashboard had a large sight drip-feed for oil, a priming pump, and a brass speedometer which registered up to 30 miles per hour. The tyres were beyond hope, but here I was in luck. I was amazed to find that they were the same size as the beaded-edge covers which had been fitted to my old G.N.s, and I had plenty of them at home.

I had brought some petrol with me, and soon, after some vigorous swinging, the engine sprang to life, and ran as sweetly as on the day it was made.

As the engine seemed to need no tuning, the preparation of the car consisted of much polishing of brass, and generally restoring the car to its original appearance. At some time it had been vandalised, and much of the brasswork had been painted over. All this paint was carefully removed, to expose the metal, and a modern horn was discarded in favour of a beautifully curved brass bulb horn found in a scrap-yard. Alas, the acetylene generator was hopelessly corroded inside, so it was impossible to restore the original lighting arrangement; but it took a nice shine, and sat in useless splendour on the nearside running board.

In the meantime, the search for old cars among other members of the motor clubs had produced amazing results, and entries for the event, which inevitably came to be known as the Old Crocks Race', soon exceeded 40. Even the vehicle which was reputed to be the first car to be driven in Scotland was brought to light, and appeared to be nothing more or less than a horse carriage with an engine under the seat, and a tiller to steer by. Many long-forgotten names such as Germaine and Argyll appeared on the list. The enthusiasm was immense, and nothing else was discussed at the various club gatherings.

It had been decided that the event would be less austere than the Emancipation Run counterpart in England, and intending competitors were encouraged to dress in period clothing. Thus, not only were old cars in demand, but attics were being ransacked, and theatrical stores searched for deerstalker caps, dust veils, and frock coats. Lady passengers who could hunt out suitable attire were much in demand.

Two days before entries were due to close my brother, Jock, came home on leave, and immediately became infected with this strange urge to obtain and drive a veteran car. But the likely sources had been well scoured by this time, and there seemed little hope of making a fresh discovery. Then I remembered dimly that many years before I had seen a very old car at a farm auction some miles away. It was worth following up, so we set off at once and soon found the little farm in the hills. The new owner did not remember anything about it, but a farm hand, true to type in remembering everything that has happened in his parish for 20 years, put us on the trail again. A farmer had bought it at the auction, and in his turn had sold it to another farmer who lived a couple of miles further into the hills. We thanked him and set off again, and at our next call we located our quarry and its present owner. Yes, he had bought the car, but it had been no use to him and he had dismantled it. Indeed, a brief look round his yard showed us the truth of this statement. There was the chassis, supporting a rick of hay; the front axle had been converted into a rough trailer; there was the body, tastefully arranged as a sort of garden seat. The petrol tank was used to store his lamp oil.

The situation seemed hopeless, but the old farmer seemed to like the opportunity of getting all the old junk out of his yard. He assured us that he could lay his hands on all the parts, and if we could get him another axle for his trailer, and another tank to put his paraffin oil in, we could have the whole lot—for a pound.

We returned that evening with a lorry, and sure enough, the farmer had collected everything in a heap, even down to a jam jar of nuts and bolts, and the trembler coils which he had preserved on top of the kitchen dresser. In a short time all was loaded up and in due course unloaded in my yard, and the next day the Leinster Club received as an additional entry, one 1911 two-seater Model T Ford.

It would be as well to pass over the next few days, during which the rusty, dirt-caked parts were being assembled. It is sufficient to state that at the end of a week the old car was on its wheels again, and after some lengthy towing, the engine started and it ran under its own power. As the bodywork was quite beyond hope as far as restoration was concerned, Jock decided that he would go to the other extreme and the car would be run exactly as it was-rust, dirt and all. It was exactly like something out of one of the old Keystone comedy films; the upholstery sprouted horsehair, water spouting from all parts of the radiator, doors tied on with rope, and as a nice finishing touch, a spare crankshaft protruded from the enormous tool box.

The great day eventually arrived, warm and sunny, and our ill-assorted convoy set out for the start. The Renault, with sparkling brasses and whitened tyres, its crew turned out correctly in the clothes of the period; the Ford, rusty and rattling, smoke rising from the noisy engine, its driver dressed in Charlie Chaplin style, battered bowler hat, frock coat, and large boots.

The Model T Ford and the two-cylinder Renault, both of about 1911. The brothers discussing the prospects of what spectators insisted on calling a 'race'.

The competing cars were lined up in a vast garage which had been put at the disposal of the club by the omnibus company, and from here they set out on the 20-mile journey, one by one, through an enormous crowd which had turned out to witness this first run of the 'Old Crocks'. Driving under these conditions was extremely hazardous, as the ordinary spectators had no idea of the difficulties in controlling these old cars, with steering and brakes none too effective. The people jammed the entire width of the road, and only moved back to expose a narrow lane at the last possible moment. Out in the country things were a little easier, but we were menaced by the drivers of modern cars who cut in and out among the veterans, often stopping suddenly right in front of a brakeless monster.

The route was through slightly hilly country on the outskirts of Dublin, through the holiday resort of Bray, and finishing at the seaside town of Dun Laoghaire, where the cars were lined up on the promenade, again amidst vast crowds. Each group of cars, divided according to age, was expected to average a certain speed, and I think the 1911 class was expected to maintain 15 m.p.h. The Renault and the Ford had no difficulty in accomplishing this, and we both completed the course well on time, so much so that I found that I had won the first prize in my class, and was duly presented with the handsome Semper Idem Cup.

The whole outing is now one gloriously happy memory. Everyone, whether competitor, official, or spectator, was in the highest spirits. The crowd laughed with, rather than at, the old machines and their crews, while the more serious minded could ponder on the theme of the development of the automobile. I look back on that first Veteran Car Run as one of the most enjoyable adventures of my life.

CHAPTER XXII.
The Midgets

IT will be obvious to any reader who has persevered thus far with these writings that my motoring was hampered throughout by a lack of funds. Not that this shortage was in any way unusual in a young man not long out of college, but unfortunately my impecuniosity was entirely disproportionate to my enthusiasm for the sport.

It was this combination of opposites that made me reach the conclusion that, if I could not afford motor sport, then motor sport would have to be adapted to suit my finances.

My idea was to build a racing car of very small size and moderate power from all the bits and pieces of cars and motor-cycles that littered the yard here, to persuade a few enthusiasts to do the same, and then to find a suitable track on private ground within easy reach. It seemed to me that if these things could be done a great deal of fun could be had at very small expense. I had, of course, heard of 'midget car racing' in America, although I did not realise at the time that it was a highly developed professional sport, and I had also heard vague reports of a small band of enthusiasts in the Bristol area who were doing just what I had in mind with some success.

Once this idea had taken a firm hold there was little hope of resisting it. I put my proposition before some of my more ardent friends, and it was received with varying degrees of enthusiasm. Some were willing to build, but wished to have some assurance that there would be enough similar machines to make competition; others wanted to see a suitable track prepared before building the cars. In effect, there was a form of deadlock, with all the intending competitors playing a waiting game, hoping for someone else to commit himself first.

There was nothing for it, but that I should build a car myself in the hopes that it would encourage others; and as soon as I had made this decision I set about the business of collecting together all the necessary parts, and in this respect I was extremely lucky in that I had a sizeable assortment of portions of discarded Austins, G.N.s, motor-cycles, and even motor mowers from which to choose.

One of the first things to be decided, when setting out to design an entirely new class of vehicle, is the formula to which it will be built. Without this, future builders would have no guide and their creations might have no resemblance in appearance or performance to the original. Normally this formula would be drawn up by an earnest panel of technicians, probably with national or even international powers. In my case, I was playing a lone hand and I had to decide the formula for myself.

The most important point in this new formula for 'midget cars' was the limitation to be placed on engine size, and after much deliberation I decided that the best source of power would be a large single cylinder motor-cycle engine. Anything larger would entail using a car engine which would be heavy and difficult to install in a very small chassis, while anything smaller would not have sufficient power to give results on four wheels. I therefore laid down the maximum engine capacity to be 500 c.c.

In order that the car would be as small as practicable, it would be necessary to limit the wheelbase, and after much drawing and measuring I concluded that a suitable length would be five feet. These two limitations would be sufficient to keep any machines that might be built reasonably similar in character, and would leave plenty of scope for individual design, depending on the material available.

The provision of suitable road wheels was a big problem, as normal car wheels would be very much out of proportion on such a small vehicle. This was solved when one of the tyre manufacturers produced a very robust wheel and tyre, designed primarily for agricultural trucks and barrows, approximately on the right scale and at a ridiculously low price. I ordered four of these, outwardly for use on the farm but with every intention of incorporating them in my embryo racer.

Having decided to build, and having set my own limitations as to construction, it became necessary to find a suitable engine. I remembered that my erstwhile college friend, Harry Carson, had once borrowed a powerful motor-cycle with a view to rebuilding it as a racing machine, but had not found time to work at it. It was not long before I had in turn borrowed this machine from him, and in a very short time, having removed its engine, I found that here was just the type of unit for my purpose. It was a very fine Blackburne with overhead valves, which, I believe, had been designed for power and speed of a racing order. The work of fitting this engine in a very much cut-down G.N. chassis proceeded apace, and in a very few weeks my first midget car began to take shape. Needless to say, plenty of unexpected snags cropped up during the assembly, and sometimes I found myself despairing of making a satisfactory job.

While I was patiently hammering and sawing away at my new toy, rumour reached me that I was not alone in this peculiar enthusiasm. Somebody had heard of somebody who lived on the other side of Dublin who was doing much the same thing. Of course I set off as soon as possible to track down this soul-mate; and it was not long before I discovered him, actually working at his creation in the garage attached to his suburban house, while his staid saloon stood forlorn in the cold of the garden.

By the greatest luck, or coincidence, my new acquaintance, Mr. Flood, had fixed on the same formula as I had chosen. His car, fitted with the famous Scott two-stroke engine, had reached about the same stage of development as my own, and it looked like a really workmanlike job. We exchanged ideas and criticisms freely, and both afterwards attacked our machines with renewed vigour. There was real competition at last.

Mr. Flood had succeeded in inspiring one or two others, and I soon discovered two other cars under construction. These were being constructed by young men who had had no previous experience of motor sport, which was probably the reason why I had never met them. Mr. Flood had not been involved in motor sport either, and approached it from quite a different angle. He had been a keen competitor in motor boat races of the outboard hydroplane type, and had conceived the idea of transferring this type of sport to dry land. He hoped to race his car on the sands, or on a level sports field. That would suit me perfectly.

With four cars under construction, and a number of people thoroughly interested, the time had come to 'get organised'. A meeting was held, and I soon found myself with the not altogether enviable job of honorary secretary of the 'Dublin Midget Racing Car Club', which was the title we gave ourselves. It only remained now to perfect the cars and to hold races. Or so it seemed.

But plans—especially motor racing plans—never seem to follow the straightforward course, and here was no exception. One of our four hopefuls developed a fault in the very fundamentals of its transmission and was likely to need redesigning. Another, although well built, was of most peculiar design, resembling an advanced agricultural machine, rather than a racer. When tested it proceeded at a fast crawl, with much clanging and whirring of chains, and its appearance was not improved when its owner decided to paint it the traditional agricultural red and green. So our hoped-for field of four was reduced to two, with a possible third.

RACING IN MINIATURE
Midget cars on a cinder track. The author passes Leo Mulvanny (No 12). Both cars started life as Austin Seven saloons.

I am glad to say that both Mr. Flood's Scott and my Blackburne were quite successful and showed great promise. I was delighted with the acceleration and road-holding of my little machine, but I found myself well and truly back in the 'chain gang'. What with a motor-cycle engine at the front, a gearbox in the middle, and a G.N. back axle, the whole centre portion of my car seemed to he a mass of writhing chains which would fly off at the slightest provocation. Nevertheless, we indulged in some unofficial but highly diverting 'dicing' in a field on my farm, and we even went so far as to stage a demonstration race in connection with a grass-track event run by one of the local motor-cycle clubs. This was perhaps a mistake, as our cars were so few in number, and being rather difficult to start, did not give the best impression to the followers of this sport.

Later on in the season I thought it would be fun to drive my tiny car in one of the speed events run near Dublin for the benefit of those who wanted to try out their cars over a timed quarter-mile. One such event was scheduled to take place on a straight piece of road near the seaside village of Donabate, and having sent in my entry, I duly turned up at the start with my midget on a trailer which I had hastily constructed a few days before. My unusual machine created something of a sensation among the drivers of sports and racing cars present, who had never seen anything like it. Even the press photographers were impressed and many pictures were taken, posed beside the bigger machines, which was very good publicity for our little club.

I was more concerned about how the car would perform in front of this rather sceptical audience, and it was in some trepidation that I got ready for my first run down the course. When I got the signal to go I was pushed off by helpful friends, the engine fired at once and I set off on the half-mile run which was allowed before entering the timed quartermile section. The car accelerated nicely, and I had just got it wound up to nearly maximum speed when there was a horrid scrunch from underneath, and we free-wheeled to a halt with a broken chain. Rather shamefacedly I pushed the car off the course and proceeded to assess the damage, which could be done quite easily by tipping it over on its side. Yes, one chain had broken, but there seemed to be no other damage, so I had no trouble in effecting a hasty repair. I then manipulated the chain adjusters until the links were stretched as tight as possible, and set the car down on its wheels. Then, when the competitors were returning to the start for another run, I started off with the aid of a push from nearby spectators, and was soon back and ready for another attempt.

This time all went well, and we bounded down the course in great style, the engine revving nicely but the over-tight chain grinding and protesting under the strain. The road was none too smooth, and I was having some difficulty in holding the car straight, which was not surprising, as it was almost devoid of any form of springing and weighed something under four hundredweight. I kept a wary eye on the tyres, which had been designed for the better type of wheelbarrow, and probably had not been intended to travel at more than five m.p.h. But everything stayed together, and I flashed through the timed section, gently slowing up to join the waiting competitors at the finish.

When we got back to the control end of the course I was informed that my speed had been just under 55 m.p.h., which was quite as much as I had hoped for, and was also good enough to win for me the handicap prize. I took my little car home, well satisfied with its performance.

....

The appearance of our midget cars had evoked interest in the most unexpected places, hut nevertheless I was rather surprised when I was approached by the local veterinary surgeon. This gentleman was interested in the sport of trotting ponies, and it was his intention to run a meeting on the next bank holiday. He felt, however, that he might not be able to collect a sufficient number of ponies to make up a day's racing, and he had conceived the idea of running races for midget cars in conjunction with them.

Now, it seemed to me that: trotting ponies and midget cars would not make the best mixture, but we were anxious to race anywhere before the public, so I accepted his offer with enthusiasm. I immediately notified the other car-owning members, and they acclaimed the idea with joy. As I have said before, we could only muster three cars, but we were undismayed and at once got down to the job of preparing our machines.

I had assumed that a track that was suitable for the light gigs used by the trotting fraternity would also suit our midgets, but when the day arrived and we turned up at the chosen venue near Dundrum we were rather taken aback. Here was a large and bumpy field which had only recently been vacated by a herd of badly trained cows. It was crossed here and there by deep drains, which had been roughly filled in with earth where they actually crossed the oval track, which was marked out with stakes and rope. There seemed to be no means of controlling the spectators who were already beginning to roll up in their thousands.

The meeting, as is usual on these occasions, started about an hour behind schedule with some preliminary heats for the ponies. These went according to plan, until the driver of the Scott-engined midget was incautious enough to start his engine for testing, when two of the more highly-strung animals took charge of their drivers and disappeared from the field at full gallop. In due course the time for our race arrived, and the three little cars were wheeled out on to the starting line.

At the drop of the flag, the Scott midget took the lead while I bumped along some yards behind. Bringing up the rear was the third car, looking more like an agricultural implement than ever in the rural setting, and at a pace rather better than the average lawn mower. I was having transmission and chain trouble on the fearsome bumps and did not dare to apply full power. Four laps were covered in this way, and the Scott passed the post an easy winner. The bookmakers, and there were scores of them, had offered approximately even odds on all the cars and now cheerfully paid out on the winner.

Later in the programme came our second race, and the three cars again appeared on the line. This time I had tightened the chains until the chassis was strained like a drawn bow, and I intended to make a race of it or bust. Owing to our performance in the first event, the Scott was now hot favourite, my car stood at about ten to one, and the third car was rank outsider. The ponies were herded away to a quiet corner of the field, and the three cars were pushed into life.

Mishap at Dundrum.

This time my car was going really well, and I soon had a commanding lead. After two laps I eased off a bit, and then found that the Scott had found some more speed and was gaining rapidly. I found it necessary to open up a bit, and I was just taking a cautious look rearward when disaster overcame me. The car hit an unusually large bump, and slid sideways. Next minute the little wheels had dug into the soft ground—and crash, over we went. Over and over again, while I saw nothing but instantaneous flashes of sky and earth, while bits of the car and the contents of my pockets flew out in every direction. Eventually we came to rest, upsidedown, but more or less unhurt.

As I kicked off the remains of the car and struggled to my feet I saw that the crowd had lost interest in the race and were rushing towards me. At the same time the Scott midget came to rest nearby and I assumed the driver had stopped to render assistance. Later I found that his stop was entirely involuntary owing to unusual circumstances. It appears that the carburettor, which was placed perilously near the person of the driver in that tiny car, had sucked his handkerchief out of his pocket and had absorbed it into the works, thereby causing a complete stoppage.

Then the crowd suddenly woke up to the fact that most of its money was on the Scott. They lost interest in me and there was much shouting and gesticulating as it was quite ineffectively urged to finish the race. In the meantime the driver of the third car, quite unperturbed by all the excitement, whirred and ground his way slowly round the course, eventually to be declared the winner.

So ended the first public performance of this new venture, midget car racing. It could well have ended there, but from these small beginnings grew a sport which has taken a firm place among the motoring events in this country.

The further development of the sport is outside the scope of these notes; but as I look back on those early days I am infused with a glow of satisfaction at having helped to inaugurate a venture which was to bring motor racing within the grasp of many who would not otherwise have been able to indulge.

CHAPTER XXIII.
Cork

WHEN the rains and mud of winter began to give precedence to the sunshine of early spring in 1938 the season of speed events was on us, and my thoughts inevitably turned to the possibility of competing in another big road race.

At this time some high officials of the national sweepstake organisation had begun to take an interest in motor racing, and they had allotted a large sum of money for a meeting of international importance to be held outside the City of Cork. All the big names in continental Grand Prix racing were to be invited, handsome prize and starting money being put up as an attractive inducement.

The programme of the 1938 International Race meeting in Cork
-courtesy of RIAC Archive

The sweepstake authorities, being somewhat horse-minded, insisted that their race be dubbed 'The Irish Motor Derby', a title which the motoring fraternity had some difficulty in swallowing.

The idea was acclaimed with enthusiasm by the commercial-minded and sport-loving people of Cork, and when it was rumoured that the German Mercedes and Auto-Union teams were considering sending in entries a wave of excitement went through the whole motoring community. The French Delahayes also signified their intention to compete, and there were many enquiries from private owners of Maseratis, Bugattis, etc.

The actual running of the event was to be left in the hands of the Irish Motor Racing Club, and this body, which always endeavoured to cater for the lesser known names as well as the stars, insisted that a handicap event in which the local boys might have a chance should be run in conjunction with the big race.

As soon as the regulations governing these races reached me I realised that here was just the event to suit my Frazer Nash, which was not taking kindly to being used as a road hack. Then I looked at the required entry fee—ten guineas— and found myself up against the usual financial obstacle.

There was nothing for it but to find another sporting fairy godmother, willing to put up the entry fee and to take a gamble on the unlikely chance of winning a cash prize. Of course, there was Phyllis Godfrey still very keen on the sport in spite of her unremunerative sponsorship, but I was not sufficiently thick-skinned to ask her to do the same thing a second time.

As I cast my mind about for a fresh victim I suddenly remembered the existence of a very good friend of my family who actually lived and worked in the Cork area, and though not heretofore particularly interested in motor racing, he had been deeply involved in other forms of mechanical sport. He had owned a light aeroplane, and had in fact expended a great deal of his time and money in helping to keep a flying club going in his district. This was one Jim Gates, the manager of a big creamery concern, whose cheery grin, all-enveloping bonhomie, and unbounded energy made him a popular figure wherever sportsmen gathered in the South of Ireland.

Now, aeroplanes and those who fly them have always been associated in my mind with money and a sporting instinct; therefore who could be more suitable as a possible backer than Jim Gates? All I wanted was a paltry ten pounds or so and the fun of the race; he would be welcome to any prize money I might collect. Perhaps if I had thought there was the slightest possibility that I might win any money prize I might not have been so free with these sweeping propositions; but the idea that I might do anything other than have some fun and maybe finish intact just never occurred to me.

All that was now needed was for me to summon up enough nerve to ask Jim, and finally after much pen-chewing I concocted a long and involved letter setting out my proposition. I posted it with a silent prayer, and began to wait impatiently for an answer. Indeed, the answer came much sooner than I expected and my heart bumped when I heard and recognised Jim's voice on a long-distance call the very next evening.

"I've been thinking over your letter," said the voice, "and I'd like to help, but not on your terms. I'll pay half of all expenses connected with the race, and I'll expect half of any winnings that may come our way. Think it over, and if you agree keep in touch with me and let me know what will be wanted to get the car ready."

Before he had rung off I had made up my mind, and I knew that somehow I would have to find the other half of the expenses. On the next day, for the second time in my life, I was filling in an entry form for a race meeting of international importance.

When Mick Burke, my garage owning and unpaid mechanic friend, heard the news he was beside himself with joy. He had regarded my every-day use of the Frazer Nash with strong disapproval, and considered that it should be kept for races and speed events only. He now took it away from me almost by force and started right away to dismantle it for a thorough overhaul; and there began a period of sleepless nights and hectic week-ends as the work of preparing the car proceeded. Again many an innocent customer bringing his family saloon to the garage for repair was gruffly sent away and told to come back in about a month. Everything was checked and rechecked, and every worn part was replaced, and finally Mick stood back and declared that the car was as right as he could make it. I must admit that when I took it down the road on test I found it hard to believe that it was still powered by the twelve horse power engine that had been taking me about my business through the winter.

Preparation for a race does not end with the tuning of the car, and as the big day drew near I made all the other arrangements that become necessary when competing far from home. We would have to remain in the race area for three or four days to cover the practice period, and we would have to find somewhere to sleep and to garage the car. Here Mick Burke was a help, as he was acquainted with an undertaker in Cork city, and he arranged that the car would be housed in the funeral establishment—a bizarre notion which tickled his sense of humour. For myself, I was lucky in that my cousin, Elizabeth Bowen, who was involved in an adventure earlier in these writings, was the owner of a large country house near Cork, which she had kindly placed at my disposal, only regretting that she would not herself be present. As a result of this generous offer, I became possessed by the idea of doing the race in the grand manner, and with the aid of my eldest sister we set about organising a house party of motoring friends and their womenfolk to support us and to join in any celebrations that might be laid on in connection with the races. This was a happy thought, and we brought to motor racing something of the spacious atmosphere that attended the big country house parties that went with the more famous horse race meetings in days gone by. As the genial Jim Gates lived only a mile away, conditions were set fair for a very pleasant sojourn in the South.

While the car was being prepared for the race, Mick Burke's garage on the main road became a centre of interest. News quickly spread that it was an entrant in the big Cork race, and indeed this was not surprising as the Frazer Nash in all its starkness had pride of place in the centre of the floor, near the door for all to see. Night after night a cluster of enthusiasts would gather round to talk motor cars and to discuss the prospects of the race. Among these was a young man, Don Roche, who made himself so useful that Mick decided he would be a good choice to help with the pitwork during the race; and Don was so delighted with this prospect that he offered me the use of his own car as a means of personal transport for the race period, provided he could travel down to Cork in the Frazer Nash. I accepted with alacrity, and found myself driving about in a very snappy M.G. Magna while the Nash was in the sole charge of Mick Burke.

I now felt I was on even terms with all the well-to-do competitors who roll up to races in expensive sports cars, while their racers follow on in large covered vans, watched over by teams of zealous mechanics. I had my racer, my team of mechanics and my hack car, and I would not have changed places with 'Bira' himself.

Three days before race day we loaded our cars with all manner of tools and spare parts and set out in convoy for the South. The trip was uneventful, but for one rather disquieting mishap. Twenty miles from Cork we came on the Frazer Nash stopped beside the road with a broken driving chain. This was all the more unnerving because we had just fitted a complete new set of chains of reputable manufacture, and there did not seem to be any reason for the failure. If chains were going to break while running lightly on the public road, what was going to happen in the race? There was nothing else to be done but to fit a new link and to carry on as before.

Having arrived in Cork we attended the very strict scrutiny, which included a medical examination of the driver, and then the car was taken round to the Dunlop factory where it was fitted with a brand new set of racing tyres, an item which Jim Gates had insisted upon. Then it was taken to its funeral establishment billet, and after a thorough check-over, it was left in peace until the first practice period, which was to take place at the grim hour of six o'clock on the following morning.

'Bira' raced the Maserati in the Cork Grand Prix.

That evening the entire City of Cork seemed to have been given over to the business of motor racing. One of the principal hotels had been adopted as race headquarters, and judging by the number of motor racing types to be seen in the halls and lounges' there can have been little room for the ordinary residents. Every garage had its quota of racing cars, all surrounded by gaping crowds as last minute repairs and final check-overs were carried out. At every street corner raucous voices proclaimed the sale of programmes.

Practice for Johnny Wakefield's Maserati. Frazer Nash in background

Long before daybreak a solid stream of traffic, intermingled with snarling racing cars, was on the way out to the course, and I reached the paddock area to find Mick Burke and my Frazer Nash ready and waiting, engine nicely warmed up. As the last of the morning mist melted away, and the grey light of dawn gave place to cheerful sunshine, the faster cars were sent away for the first practice period. The organisers had wisely decided to

Grand Prix winner Dreyfus in the Delahaye.

segregate the out-and-out Grand Prix cars from the slower machines so that there would not be cars of widely differing speed capabilities on the course at the same time. As it happened, the list of Grand Prix entries was not as imposing as had been hoped, as the famous Mercedes and Auto-Union cars had failed to materialise. Nevertheless, there were many famous names on the course that morning, including Wimille, Dreyfus, Commotti, 'Bira'. As I watched these cars come down the long straight at speeds in excess of 130 m.p.h., I was glad to be in the paddock and did not grudge them this first hour of the practice.

Then came my turn, and having been given the signal to go, I set off round the course on my first cautious lap.

The Cork course is very roughly D shaped, with a fine, long straight of almost three miles, dead level. This was the road which had been used some years before for attacks on world motor-cycle records. The rest of the course was rather narrow, twisty and undulating, with one very sharp hairpin where speeds would be reduced to the twenties. At the end of the straight there was a right angled corner, and the road at this point was very wide. I found this particularly hard to judge, and even on my first lap I found myself sliding wildly outwards. This would have to be watched, as it presented an ideal opportunity for a rival to slip by on the inside.

Practice for the author - number plate yet to be removed.

As the car seemed to be running perfectly and there was no cause to stop for adjustments, I gave the 'O.K.' signal to my pit and settled down to learn the course. I concentrated on the intricate curves of the 'back leg' and rested the engine on the long straight. There was nothing to be learnt by going flat out on a straight road. The signal to end the practice period came all too soon, and as I handed the car back to Mick Burke I realised that I would need all of the next day's practice to familiarise myself with the course. I made up my mind to spend the rest of the day driving round at moderate speed in the borrowed M.G., just to learn the sequence of the bends. These intentions were somewhat upset when the driver of another Frazer Nash entry found pieces of whitemetal in his sump oil, and I felt obliged to spend some time in helping him to strip his engine.

Later in the day, when the evening papers appeared, I was startled to find my name among those doing well on handicap, and tipped as a possible winner. Up to this moment such a thing had never entered my head, but now a thrill of excitement went through me at the thought of possible success. I began to take things more seriously.

Next morning we arrived at the course for practice to find it enveloped in fog. This threatened to cut into the time allowed for practice, but after a delay of half-an-hour the sun began to break through. Soon I was out on the course, and determined to learn every bend and bump before the 'all in' flag. I had completed one lap and was coming down the straight on the second when I found myself straining to listen to the note of the engine. Was that a slight miss? A minute later there was no doubt; there was an intermittent misfire at high revs.

I pulled into my pit and informed Mick. Out came all the plugs and in with a new set. Off again, but before I reached the first corner I realised there was no improvement. Back in the pits on the next time round we checked everything we could think of, but still the miss persisted. I decided to keep going till the end of the practice, to learn the road; we had the rest of the day to find the trouble. Although I put in several more laps I am afraid I did not learn much of the course, as I could not concentrate while the engine was running uncomfortably.

A highly agitated Mick Burke took the car back to its temporary garage, and immediately whipped off the magneto. Here undoubtedly was the trouble, but what could we do about it? A hectic rush round all the garages in Cork soon proved that we would not get a spare in that city. The afternoon was spent in frantically wiring to all the known electrical dealers in Dublin, but reply after reply came back: "No suitable magneto in stock!"

Late that evening, as black despair was descending on our crew, a telegram arrived from a well-known Dublin firm which had helped us on more than one occasion:

"HAVE LOCATED CUSTOMER'S MAGNETO SUITABLE FOR NASH. DISPATCHING CORK NIGHT TRAIN. GOOD LUCK."

An enquiry at the station revealed that the only possible train would reach Cork at 5.30 on the following morning. Nothing to be done but to possess our souls in patience and to hope for the best.

There was little sleep for me that night, and none at all for Mick Burke, who was at the station when the train was still 40 miles away. Mick was in the parcels van before the train had properly stopped, and in a very few minutes he was back at our base, clutching the precious magneto. Yes, it would fit all right, but it was of a different type to the faulty instrument and would need an entirely different bracket. This would have to be made up in the short time available from locally obtained material.

All that morning, the morning of the race, was spent in fabricating a rough but effective bracket in a garage near the undertaker's yard. The magneto was finally fitted, and the engine roughly timed, shortly before we were due to appear in the paddock near the starting line. There was no time to try out the car or to make accurate adjustments to the timing: these things had to be left to chance.

We were busy trying to organise our pit-counter into some sort of order when instructions came to take up position. We pushed the car out and lined it up on the grid. Loud speakers raucously ordered all drivers to assemble for briefing by the clerk of the course, Major MacNeill. We stood in a group, trying to concentrate on what he was saying, while our eyes strayed to the road stretching down to the first corner. "Pass on the left, watch out for blue flags, if the car stops pull right off the road." Would he never stop? Out of the corner of my eye I could see my pit. Jim Gates, beaming as usual; Don Roche, clutching his lap sheet; Mick Burke, with the expression of a hen whose only chicken has strayed on to the road. ". . . look out for oil on the road. . . do one more lap after the chequered flag . . . any questions? Well, good luck, boys. Back to your cars."

Back in my car on the starting grid there was a minute or two to look round at my handicap position. Behind me were two supercharged M.G.s and the English Frazer Nash. These must be kept behind at all costs. Immediately in front, and with a half-minute start, was the incredible Morris Minor engined machine of Davy Yule; he had been the winner of my first race in the Phoenix Park. In front again was an assortment of machines, and among them Charlie Manders's neat single seater Adler. These I must pass—some of them twice—if I was to gain the lead. As the minute signal went all engines were started, and in the deafening roar I had to keep an eye on my own revolution counter. Down went the flag for the first group, then the second. As the leaders disappeared round the first corner the flag swept down again, and I was away in hot pursuit.

On that first lap I seemed to have the course to myself. There wasn't a car in sight and I had a peculiar feeling of loneliness in spite of the thousands of spectators lining the road. It was some time before I realised that the car seemed to be going better than ever with its borrowed magneto. On the second time round I passed a luckless local driver drawn in to the side of the road, bonnet up. On the third lap as I passed the pits I caught a glimpse of my pit and Mick Burke's tense face. Three pits down the line a Riley was in trouble. Bad luck, but for me—two less between me and a win.

Next time round I caught a momentary glimpse of a cream coloured tail vanishing round a curve just ahead. I was gaining on Davy Yule. Bit by bit, the distance between us lessened; then we swept on to the long straight, and the little car began to grow smaller. He had more speed on the straight, but was losing to me on the twisty part of the course where his three-speed gearbox was a heavy disadvantage. Five laps behind us now, and I was right on his tail on the back stretch. On the short downhill stretch to Carigrohane Bridge I slipped by, and when we reached the main straight again I had a fair lead. But I was to need it, and out of the corner of my eye I could see the cream coloured car creeping up behind.

At the end of the straight I braked hard for the wide corner and realised that I was going too fast. Round came the tail as we slid wildly sideways on the broad tarmac. I fought the kicking wheel and wondered if I would have to pass behind the petrol pumps at the roadside garage. No, I could just make it. Safely back on the course, I saw that my wild slide had let Yule through on the inside, and I set off in pursuit again. Yule was again handicapped for want of another gear, and I caught and passed him before we reached the straight once more; but he hung on doggedly, and once or twice drew almost level and then fell back. Afterwards Davy told me that on one or two occasions he could have passed but for the wildly swinging tail of the Frazer Nash, which seemed to occupy most of the road. The peculiar cornering style of this car with its 'solid' rear axle was responsible for this, and I don't think he believed that I was deliberately trying to baulk him.

So intent had we been on our private duel, neither of us noticed that we had passed several slower cars. As I swooped down on to the long concrete straight on the last lap but one, with Davy Yule ahout a hundred yards behind, I saw Charlie Manders in the Adler ahead. Slowly we gained on him and drew level, and for about a quarter of a mile or so we travelled side by side on the dead smooth surface. Charlie, cheerful and irrepressible as ever, shouted rude things at me and shook his fist in true continental style. We were travelling at about 95 miles per hour at this point, but on the wide, straight road it did not feel more than a mile-a-minute or so.

As the Adler slowly fell back I realised that I was now in the lead. I had lost count of the number of laps covered, but as we flashed past the pits I gathered from the excited face of Mick Burke, leaning far out over the counter, that things were approaching a climax. Then, further down the road I had a momentary vision of an official picking up the chequered flag, and this seemed a sure indication that I was starting out on the last lap. Could I hold the narrow lead? Would the engine hold out? As I listened to its note I imagined all sorts of new clatters and knocks, which seemed to be growing in intensity. And Davy Yule was pressing relentlessly behind.

Too fast again into the first corner. We swung wide, and the Morris Special crept up level on the inside. If Yule got past here I might never catch him again. I gave the engine all the revs it would take in third, and inch by inch we gained until there was a clear length between. I knew I must increase this if I was to have a good enough lead to hold him off on the straight. Brake hard for the Poulavone hairpin. Round in a slither and off again on the sweep down to the straight, with Davy less than a hundred yards behind. Only two miles to go now, and dead straight. It all depends on the car now, there is nothing more I can do.

I tucked myself down in the driving seat to cut wind resistance, and kept my foot hard on the floor. In this position the noise of the engine was magnified a hundredfold, and it seemed impossible that it would not fly to pieces at any moment. Out of the corner of my eye I could see Davy's radiator creeping gradually nearer. In the far distance I could discern an official with a flag peering up the road. If everything held together we should just about make it. Past the pits and grandstands amid a flutter of waving programmes. A hundred yards to go . . . fifty. Down swept the chequered flag, and I had won. I had actually won a motor race. It just wouldn't sink in.

A glance behind showed Yule, not 20 lengths away, acknowledging the flag. It was a near thing.

LAST LAP

The Frazer Nash rounds the hairpin before the finish of the Cork Race, with Davy Yule (C.M.Y. Special) only a few yards behind.

A little way down the road I was signalled to stop. A smiling official of the Cork club stepped out with the traditional laurel wreath, which he slipped round my neck. I was handed an enormous glass of some yellow liquid, which in the excitement of the moment, and rather to the surprise of the donor, I drained to the last drop without tasting it. A hearty slap on the back, and I was sent off on the 'lap of honour' with Davy Yule and Charlie Manders, who had finished third, close behind.

I don't know whether it was the effect of the drink, or just that my head was reeling with excitement, but that extra lap was the most dangerous piece of motoring I have

Victory for the Frazer Nash in Cork 1938

ever done. I could hardly control the car, and we zig-zagged round the course ricochetting from curb to curb. I recognised many of my friends, and I wanted to stop and shake them by the hand. I wanted to get out and dance and sing. Behind me I heard many squeals of brakes as Davy tried to keep clear of my erratic progress.

Back in the paddock after this hectic lap, I was surrounded by friends, and friends who had been strangers five minutes before. Photographs were taken, and innumerable drinks profered and consumed. Jim Gates, beaming from ear to ear, almost shook my teeth out with hearty handshakes. Mick Burke almost burst while trying to pretend that it was a certainty anyway.

Believe it or not, this race was only a preliminary to the full Grand Prix affair. I watched this race with unseeing eyes, my mind in a whirl. While famous drivers struggled for victory on this circuit—my circuit—I sat and grinned and dreamed, and signed autographs for small boys who would probably lose them before they got home. To this day I couldn't tell you who won the big race.

…………………………………..

That night the City of Cork gave itself over to celebrations in which I took part in no uncertain manner. There was extensive wining, dining, and dancing and the usual presentation of silverware; I found myself in charge of the handsome O'Boyle Trophy, which was the principal award for the race. As the dawn which heralded the close of this night of gladness broke, we set out for our country house headquarters, and is still a mystery to me how we made the journey without disaster. There is, without doubt, a guardian angel that looks after the erring motorist, and this providence arranged that my hack M.G. should run out of petrol before I had got very far on the road. The trip was concluded at a safe ten miles per hour at the end of a tow-rope.

Later we returned to my home in County Dublin to find the farm en fete. I was touched to find that the farm hands had arranged a 'welcome home' party, at which I was solemnly presented with a large cake, roughly fashioned in the shape of the old Frazer Nash. My family at home had shared in the excitement of the race, which had been broadcast by the Irish radio station. The commentator at one of the worst corners had been Barry Mason, who was well acquainted with the peculiar cornering style of my car, and he had not spared himself in giving a lurid word-picture of the incidents at his viewpoint. My mother and sister had sat by the radio in a state of tension, furiously knitting, while Bridget, the old cook, alternately dropped to her knees in devout prayer for my safety, and jumped up wildly cheering as my progress was described. At the end of the race my sister found herself with a knitted sock—two feet long!

CHAPTER XXIV.
More Road Racing

WHEN life became more or less normal again I reviewed my position with regard to future events. When my contract with Jim Gates, who had taken a very generous and liberal view of our monetary arrangement, had been squared up I found that I had quite a useful little sum in hand. In fact, barring accidents, there was enough to allow for entry in two or three races on my own account, and there might be a little left over to buy a hack car. If I intended to race seriously it would be foolish to run the Frazer Nash for every-day affairs, so a second car would be an essential, and I certainly intended to race seriously.

A lucky break occurred when I got the opportunity to buy a trials special which had been constructed by one of the old hands at the game, Paddy Le Fanu. Paddy had had more than his share of successes in both motor-cycle and car sport when I was still thinking in terms of two-stroke motor-bikes, and even to-day he is among the leaders in the trials world. He ran a small garage, and had a habit of running up cars of the special type, apparently with the object of practising the art of gas welding. One of these, based on Morris Cowley, Riley, and Lea Francis parts, was offered for sale; and I bought it at a price that would not pay for a pair of tyres for it to-day. I rebuilt this car, with some of my own so-called 'improvements'; and ran it in several trials, in which I could hold my own with other competitors. It could be described as the forerunner of the modern trials special, but it had certain snags which I was never able to overcome. The brake gear was so arranged that it invariably became inoperative after the first rocky outcrop encountered, and I would find myself finishing a trial without any proper means of stopping. On one such occasion, when driving without brakes, a steering arm broke and I travelled several hundred yards without any means of control before hitting a wall head-on. However, Le Fanu had constructed the chassis with such eventualities in mind, and very little damage was done.

I entered the Frazer Nash in two more international races that season, the Leinster Trophy and the Phoenix Park.

The start of th1938 Leinster Trophy at Tallaght with Charlie Mander's Adler 'Einsitzer'

These races passed off without incident and I qualified as a finisher in both. In these notes I have endeavoured to avoid descriptions of events which follow the normal pattern, and it is for this reason that I do not intend to attempt what has been done by far abler pens than mine. It does not imply that I enjoyed the races any less.

One result of the season's fun is that I can add to my list of well-known drivers who have passed me at speed several times in the same race. These include Tony Rolt, Robin Hanson, Billy Cotton, 'Taso' Mathieson, and the late St. John Horsfall.

Billy Cotton's ERA and a BMW at the Phoenix Park 1938.

The rare Multi-Union of Staniland in the 'Park 1938

At the end of the 1938 season it had become obvious that there was not much more to be got out of the Frazer Nash in its sports car form. The handicappers had it well 'taped', and unless drastic alterations were made I could only look forward at best to a series of finisher's awards. I therefore decided that the time had come to turn it into an out-and-out racer. This would entail considerable lightening and the fitting of a single-seater body. Throughout the winter we worked on this job in Mick Burke's chilly garage, and when spring came the old car appeared, completely transformed and weighing well under twelve hundredweight. Out amateur efforts at body building were not exactly handsome, but the frontal area had been almost halved, and a long tail projected out behind. It was in this form that I entered for the Leinster International Trophy for the second time.

Single Seater bodied Frazer Nash at Tallaght-1939 Leinster Trophy.

Readers who have stayed with me thus far will gain the impression that all motor sport is a joyous and lighthearted affair. Obviously this could not always be so, and this account of the 1939 Leinster Trophy will demonstrate that there is very definitely a grimmer side.

The morning of the race was ominously dull and cloudy, and by the time we were arranged on the starting grid a steady downpour had started. Miserable spectators huddled together in the open grand-stand, and the personnel in the pits endeavoured to keep their lap sheets from becoming wet pulp. At the drop of the flag we rushed off down the straight in a flurry of spray, cars in front appearing as a blur on the road. I had not driven my car in its lightened form on wet roads before, and it felt extremely unstable and liable to slide its tail round without warning. Visibility through a wet visor was very poor, but as I wore glasses I would be worse off if I discarded it.

Nearing the end of the first lap, I had my first shock. Glancing to the left on a slight bend I was horrified to see a jagged hole in a high wire fence; and in the field beyond was a car, out of control and travelling in a wide circle, with the driver lolling over the wheel. Frantic officials were giving chase, or trying to board the moving vehicle. And then the scene passed out of my vision, leaving me with a horrible feeling in the pit of my stomach, and wondering what could have happened. Next time round an ambulance was in the field, and things seemed to be under control, but there was no way of knowing the fate of the driver. Later I heard that it was McClure of Belfast, who had touched the wall with a hubcap and had got out of control. He had been knocked unconscious and badly cut about the face by the mesh wire, and the car, a $3^1/_2$ S.S. (the forerunner of the present miraculous Jaguar), had eventually come to rest against the stump of a tree. McClure made a good recovery and was back in the game in a couple of months.

The race continued, and I struggled with the sliding, skating car at very much reduced speed. Then another unpleasant shock. On the back stretch I had a glimpse of a green radiator sticking out through the hedge at a grotesque angle, bearing the number 12. My heart seemed to stick in my throat as I realised that this was the number of Paddy Le Fanu's special, which had a similar engine to that in my car. An accident to any driver in a race is a disheartening occurrence, but when it happens to a personal friend all joy is robbed from the event. I had to face the rest of the race in uncertainty, and with no desire to continue. Later, when I called to my pit, I found that my confused mind had misread the number on the crashed car. The number was 21 upside down, and Paddy was still in the running. The driver involved had not been injured.

As the laps went by I had the feeling that I was driving far slower than my rivals. I could imagine expressions of derision on the faces of scornful spectators as I slowed for the slippery bends, yet the car felt at its safe limit. When later on I was passed on a fast bend by a small car that seemed to be mainly Morris Minor I decided that I must improve my pace if I was not to be disgraced. Coming out of the sharp turn at Templeogue Bridge I used the throttle just a little bit more than my instinct told me was enough, and in the next moment I was in a wild slide, which ended with violent contact with the high curb. The result was a badly buckled wheel, some rents in the body, and a large piece of concrete removed from the curb. Incidentally, this curbstone is in the same condition to-day, and serves as a reminder to me not to play tricks with my own judgement.

I got the car going and crawled round to my pit on a very wobbly wheel, which took more than ten minutes to remove as the hub had become warped. I set off again with some idea of finishing the race some time, but two laps later I was enveloped in a cloud of hot water and steam when a radiator hose, presumably loosened by the violent jar, came adrift from its connection. The effort of propelling the car to the pit again with little or no water was too much for the overworked engine, and I forthwith retired from this unhappy contest.

Later on, when lap times were examined, I found that my pace had not been too disgraceful, and in fact if I had kept going at my own set speed I might have finished in the first four or five. The Morris Minor affair which had upset my equilibrium was, in actual fact, a car known as the 'Himmelwagen' driven by the irrepressible Ernie Robb from Belfast. This car had been fitted with a 1,500 c.c. Alvis engine about a fortnight before the race, to such good purpose that it was the winner by a substantial margin.

As the summer of that fateful year, 1939, merged into autumn the threat of war hung heavily in the air. The Irish Motor Racing Club had an international date for a race in the Phoenix Park to take place on the 9th September, and they found themselves in a difficult position. The preliminary organisation of such a race costs a great deal of money, and if the race had to be called off there would be heavy financial loss; yet they were loth to abandon the event and to break the series which had run successfully for many years.

It was eventually decided to take the risk, and the organisers were gratified to receive a fair number of promised entries from England, as well as the usual support from the North of Ireland and the local boys. I was numbered among these.

But fate stepped in, and on the Sunday previous to the race day, Mr. Chamberlain made his sombre announcement from Downing Street, and half the world was at war.

The Government of Eire had elected to remain neutral in this conflict, and certainly war seemed very far removed from our country at the time. The Irish Motor Racing Club found itself with another difficult decision to make, and I think it is to its credit that it was decided to take the bold course and run the race with the support of the Irish competitors. A motor-cycle race was hastily arranged to fill up the programme, and all other plans went ahead.

The talk in the paddock before the start of the race was a curious mixture of war, politics, and motoring. There was a general air of uneasiness which made it hard to settle down to a comparatively frivolous pastime. The usual stream of spectators pouring into this popular venue seemed much smaller than usual.

For the competitors, all thoughts of everything but the race were crowded out as the starting time approached. I found myself lined up on the grid next to a beautiful little special, built from Ford and Riley parts by a well-known driver, Aubrey Thompson, of Mallow. This car was an example of the art of the enthusiast-cum-engineer, and had independent springing all round and a De Dion type rear axle. Nevertheless I was surprised, when our flag fell and we shot away together, that I was only just able to hold on to his tail for the first mile. During the summer I had been experimenting with the Frazer Nash's valve timing, and I was confident that it was going like never before.

As we settled down to the race I found that I could just stay in Thompson's slip-stream, but when I pulled out into the still air to pass I began to lose ground. For several laps we circled in this order, and I began to think that this was going to be the race of my life. As we flashed past the pits I saw a signal giving my lap time, and I had previously calculated that this time was fast enough to win. All I had to do was to stay on Thompson's tail until he blew up. But motor racing doesn't work out like that. It was not Aubrey Thompson's car which blew up.

The Nash had never gone better, and I reckon that our speed was very nearly 105 m.p.h. down the slightly curved 'back stretch'. My revolution counter was reading perilously near the safe limit, but I dare not ease off, and thereby lose touch with the Thompson special. And then, as we breasted the long straight rise to the pits, there was a sickening clonk and clatter and puff of smoke from my old engine, and we coasted to a standstill, accompanied by the metallic rattle of pieces of metal tinkling on the road behind. Aubrey Thompson disappeared in the distance, and went on to win this last international race to be held in the British Isles for more than six years.

As I examined the wreck of my beloved engine, it was again brought home to me that motor racing is not all carefree fun. I had the one consoling thought that even if I still had a fast motor car there would be no more events for some time in which to compete.

CHAPTER XXV.
The Years Between

THIS book is an account of motoring experiences, and such things have no place in a major war. I therefore only touch on this considerable portion of our young lives in so far as it affected the motoring community in and around my home.

As private motoring became more and more restricted, and was eventually banned altogether, many young men in the motor trade found themselves without a business. Many joined the rapidly expanding forces of this country, where their experience of motor-cycling and mechanical knowledge were invaluable in the transport services. Among these Stanley Woods and Manliff Barrington, two of the top-liners in the racing world, found themselves in charge of the training of large numbers of recruit dispatch riders, thereby helping to swell the number of motor-cyclists in subsequent years of peace. The more adventurous (including my brother, Jock) went across to England and joined the R.A.F. and other services.

I had to make a decision as to my own future, and after due consideration, I decided that as long as my country remained neutral I could best serve it by sticking to my calling as a producer of essential foodstuffs. I could also use my school-day military training to help organise the local Defence Force, the equivalent of the Home Guard in England. Most of my spare time was passed in this work, and as in my capacity as training officer I was allotted a motor-cycle, I never entirely severed my connection with motor vehicles.

During this dead period the motoring clubs made great efforts to keep their members together in preparation for the time when peace might come to the land. Film shows and lectures were held, and then someone hit on the bright idea of push-bike 'trials'—of all things. Most of the boys were becoming expert at this form of exercise, so it was announced that a trial would be held in the hills near Dublin. A large entry was received, and it was an amusing sight to see some of our most expert motor-cyclists straining to keep their equilibrium while negotiating rough country. An interesting point was that these trials were invariably won by the top motor-cycle men, Aubrey Archer, the reigning trials expert just before the war, being an outstanding example. As for myself, I found I was just as awkward on a foot-powered machine, and never got very far, but the unaccustomed exercise was very good for me and I never felt fitter.

Later on, when the lack of a real hobby made Saturday afternoons hang rather heavily on my hands, I was bitten with the idea of taking up horse riding. A brother-in-law who is an expert in this game obligingly supplied me with an experienced hunter, and it was not long before I was following the local harrier pack. I got a tremendous kick out of the sport, which I found was very akin to motor-cycle trials and 'scrambling', and I became so enthusiastic that I lost all the feeling of yearning for the return of motoring. I felt that, as long as no one else had cars, I did not care how long this motorless condition continued. I was never an expert rider, and I found that the thrills were inclined to be mixed with moments of abject terror. Luckily my weight precluded the possibility of riding in point-to-point races. I say luckily, because this is probably the reason that I am still alive to-day.

The weary years rolled by, and the war reached its climax, and then came peace, of a sort. Many of my friends, including my brother, Jock, had gone never to return. Others found themselves in civilian life again, and were slowly absorbed into the rapidly recovering motor trade. I found myself lifting the dust sheet from the old Frazer Nash, and considering the future.

Early in the war I had taken the trouble to replace the original body on the Nash, more to keep the parts together than for any definite reason, and it had lain in the corner of my garage, under a dust sheet, its wheels blocked clear of the ground. The single-seater body had made an admirable chicken coop, and had paid for its keep by housing several young families. When things were at their worst I had come across a Meadows engine in a Dublin scrap-yard, and having bought it at scrap price I had unhurriedly reconditioned it and placed it in the chassis. There the car lay, with only detail work and a running-in period necessary to make it fit for work again. It would never be quite the same, but there was no reason why it should not have an excellent performance.

CHAPTER XXVI.
Peace Breaks Out

EARLY in 1946 the Irish countryside began to take on a more normal appearance, as more and more private cars flooded back on to the roads, many of them showing signs of the long hibernation. Then one bright day in January I went off to the local registration office and came away with my old Frazer Nash taxed and insured and ready for the road. I was a motorist again.

This first year of the peace was a time for much pondering by those who had been involved in motor sport before the war. What would be the future of the sport? Would young men who had spent the war flying Spitfires be content to wrestle with the wheel of a car at a paltry 100 m.p.h.? It was quite a disturbing notion that at this time there would be many hundreds of young men coming on to the roads who had learnt to fly a fighter plane before they could drive a car.

I had to do some pretty deep pondering myself to decide what would be my own attitude to the sport, if and when it was resumed. I was now six years older, and half-way through my allotted span. When I looked back on those hectic seasons of intensive racing just before the war I felt that I had no regrets and would not have missed them for the world. But now, at 35, would I be prepared to face the weeks of preparation, the all-night sessions with recalcitrant engines, the suspense—if such things were offered again?

After due consideration I reached a decision of sorts, which was somewhat influenced by the fact that I no longer possessed a car with a racing engine. I would compete in any events which might be organised, but not seriously. I would use the old car for business and pleasure during the week, and if there was an event on the Saturday, well I would be there to help swell the entry.

When shortly after this decision was made, the Irish Motor Racing Club opened the ball with a sprint event at Turvey Avenue, I realised that it would have been useless to have decided otherwise. I almost automatically filled in my entry form.

I think the organising club was a little shaken by the response to this effort to promote motor sport again. Not only was a large entry with a great number of new faces received, but the crowd of spectators which turned up to watch this exceedingly dull and unspectacular form of event was far greater than that usually seen on pre-war occasions. As to my own performance, the less said the better. The old Frazer Nash signified its disapproval of being used as a hack during the week and then being expected to go fast in public, by registering a speed of 55m.p.h. over a course on which it had nearly reached the 90 mark six years before.

Other events of the 'austerity' and sprint type were run off during the season, and each received a growing entry with many new faces and names, and an ever-increasing following of spectators. The 'old hands'—those who were regular competitors before the war—became scarcer, and it came to me with quite a shock to realise that there were only some half-dozen of these still competing. It was a greater shock to realise that I was being regarded as an 'old hand' myself— I, who such a short time ago (in terms of motoring years), had been a 'boy racer' trying to break into the sport. It was a little sad to scan entry lists and programmes that did not contain such names as Charlie Manders, David Yule, Desmond McCracken, to name a few. That some of these names now appear near the top of the lists of officials is an indication that one can never perhaps get this game entirely out of the system.

Although my old Frazer Nash had ceased to be a force to be reckoned with in the field of competitive sport, it still had the look of what has become known, illogically enough, as a 'real motor car'. It was a relic of the hand-made era of fine engineering practice, and I spared no effort to pay tribute to the designer by keeping it spick-and-span and in as near to its original condition as possible. It was gratifying to note that wherever it was parked in a city street, while I was on business errands, it would invariably collect a small crowd of admirers. In fact, I must confess that on many occasions I would deliberately leave it parked in busy thoroughfares, just for the pleasure of observing the homage from a hidden doorway, and of bathing in the glow of pride of possession. An interesting comparison could be made when my Frazer Nash happened to be parked near one of the M.G. two-seaters which were becoming very popular among the sporting fraternity in Ireland and elsewhere. The two cars are very similar in general style and size, and both cars were built for the same purpose. Yet the M.G. would be ignored by the passers-by, while the Nash would have its little circle of admirers. I suppose it is the outside gear lever and brake, the plated exhaust pipes, the aero screens and large quick action filler caps—all fittings beloved to the enthusiast—that catch the eye. Incidentally, I have the greatest respect for the M.G., which is probably a much better motor car with a better performance for a smaller engine, but I have never had the least desire to own one. But M.G.s, each one almost identical with the next, are fairly plentiful; while my mind follows the line of women and hats—I am not happy unless my car is different from the others.

The season went by and many minor events, speed trials and hill-climbs were held, much in the same way as before the war. The one big difference was the absence of a road race on the motoring calendar. Rationing of petrol was still in force, and no club felt justified in sponsoring such a big undertaking, with all the risks and difficulties of organisation. I continued my half social, half sporting existence, and while I certainly enjoyed competing in each and every event I found the very much reduced performance of the old car rather galling. When winter came I drove in reliability trials, which had been revived with an even greater intensity than the speed events of the summer. Here, again, I found my name appearing very low down on the results sheets, and I would be quite pleased to be classed as a 'finisher' in events in which I had won first-class awards in other years. I cannot altogether blame my car, which has certain inherent advantages over normal machines, for this lack of success. The fact is that a new generation of extremely keen and skilful drivers had come to the fore, and it was the general improvement of the standard of trials driving that had left, me among the 'also rans'.

Perhaps I need not feel too depressed by this partial eclipse. As I write these notes I have before me the account of the Monte Carlo Rally, probably the greatest trial of all. And the first British car to finish, taking third place in the entire entry, was driven by Cecil Vard. And Cecil was one of the new young drivers who has beaten me in Irish trials with monotonous regularity.

The speed season of 1947 was well advanced when something happened which shook me out of this rather spiritless complacency.

The Leinster Motor Club decided that it was high time a road race was held. Not necessarily a full-scale affair, but possibly a series of short races for the local boys over a short course.

Now this idea of small-scale road racing had been in my own mind for many years, but I had always been too engrossed in the competitive side of the sport to have much time for organisation. My only contribution was my part in the formation of the Midget Racing Car Club, and I had always intended that this club should cater for those interested in a scaled-down version of the real thing. But of course road racing was out of the question for the midgets.

Consider the position of the ordinary spectator at a big road race of two or three hundred miles over, say, a ten-mile lap. If he has not got a ticket for the grandstand, he takes up position somewhere out on the course, at a good vantage point. For the first lap or two he is thrilled by the speed, the noise, and the colourful spectacle as the closely packed field dash past, fighting for position. I defy anyone, no matter what his temperament, to remain unmoved by this scene. But as the race progresses the excitement wanes, and from the single viewpoint nothing is seen but a never-ending procession of racing cars, all doing much the same thing, and this may go on for several hours. Unless our spectator keeps an accurate lap-sheet (in which case he won't see the race) he has no idea what is happening, or who is in the lead. One has only to drive round such a course in the latter half of any big race to see thousands of people dozing in the sun with their backs to the road, or having picnic teas, or quelling over-exuberant children, oblivious of the 'feast of speed' going on on the road.

Take the case of the driver. He has spent weeks preparing for this day, and then one short pit-stop, or one mistake at a corner necessitating the use of the slip road may mean that he has a couple of hours hard driving to do, with very little hope of gaining a place.

Now take the case of the spectator at a meeting consisting of a number of heats and finals over a course of something over one mile. He can see most of the course, and can follow any car through a race without recourse to a lap-sheet. He knows who has won the heats and who will be running in the finals. He can walk from the start to any desired vantage point. He can have the thrill of two or three racing starts in one day, and his excitement increases as the finals are fought out. As for the drivers, if they have bad luck in one event, they have a chance to make it up in another. Their cars are not over-stressed by hours of continuous high-speed driving, and they can keep track of their own positions without complicated pit-signals.

Do not get the idea that I am decrying long-distance road racing. These events are the 'real thing' and will always have the major place on the calendar.

It was Vincent O'Reilly and his wife, Toni, two of the mainstays of post-war Irish motor sport, who were given the job of finding a suitable course and of running this first 'short circuit' meeting. They searched the countryside, by car and map, and finally settled on a little triangle of roads, out on the plains of the famous Curragh, in County Kildare. This area was under the control of the army, being near the Curragh training camp, so it was necessary to get on the right side of the Commanding Officer. Once this was done many difficulties were smoothed out, and the co-operation of the army proved invaluable.

The course was ideal for novices at road racing, consisting of three straights and three hairpin bends, at which it would be difficult to get into serious trouble. The bulk of the entry would be drivers who had never previously competed in anything but a hill-climb or reliability trial.

Unfortunately for me, I became smitten down by somewhat out-of-season influenza just before this first Curragh race, and I attended it as a spectator. The old Frazer Nash stood forlornly in the car park while I found the strain of watching these highly enjoyable little races almost unbearable. I swore then and there that before another racing season opened SOMETHING WOULD HAVE TO BE DONE.

CHAPTER XXVII.
The Walter Sexton Memorial Trophy

NEXT spring, after a winter of rather unprofitable participation in reliability trials, I began to think in terms of speed again. I would try to get the Frazer Nash, whose engine was now in its 20th year, into something like its pre-war form.

But when I came to the point of ordering the necessary new parts to perform this transformation I found that they were, to use a current phrase, 'in short supply'. Mine was practically the only Frazer Nash in Ireland, so it was not surprising that its spare parts were not carried by any of the local stockists. When I tried various factors in England I was told that I might get the parts, but the delay would be from two to eighteen months.

I had no alternative but to use the existing worn parts, and to make do with what I could get, and I finally fitted the pistons with a well-known make of laminated piston ring. These rings were regarded with suspicion by many experienced motor engineers, but I found, and later on proved, that they made an excellent substitute when new pistons and rings were unobtainable.

My next worry was chains. I had been unable to find any suitable chains for many seasons, and my only set were getting to the stage when they could not be expected to stand up to racing starts and gear changes. The situation seemed hopeless, and I had almost given up my ambitious plans when the chains appeared from the most unexpected quarter. I was attending the agricultural show in Dublin in early May, and while browsing in the Machinery Paddock, I found myself staring at a length of the desired chain. It was incorporated in the works of the latest thing in reaper-and-binders on the stand of a well-known manufacturer. All that was now necessary was to go to the local agent and to buy across the counter two lengths of the chain. And at agricultural prices, too.

The author's last race in the Frazer Nash on the short circuit in the Phoenix Park.

The work of tuning went on as well as could be expected, and in due course the car was ready for the first event of the season, the Enniskerry Hill-Climb. This event was remarkable for three reasons: first, it was extremely wet; secondly, the remarkable performance of a beautifully prepared M.G., in the hands of one of the post-war drivers, Torrie Large; and thirdly, the startling debut of Joe Kelly.

Joe Kelly is the most stirring thing that has happened to Irish motor sport since the days of Birkin and Bira. He appeared 'from nowhere' and bought the very garage where I first met my friend and mechanic, Mick Burke. He is a rabid enthusiast for motor racing in the grand manner, and he brought to the Enniskerry venue a very special singleseater Riley, beautifully prepared and painted in the official Irish colours, and ornamented with no less than six carburettors. Joe had had little or no practice with this machine, which was extremely difficult to handle, and on his first run it got out of control near the top of the hill. The car hit a bank and turned over and Joe fell out. Car and driver rolled and bounced up the road, and to this day there is doubt as to which crossed the finishing line first.

Joe was quite unhurt and undaunted, and in a short time his car was ready to race again. Since then he has bought and raced a number of very fast cars culminating in the latest Formula A Alta, with which he has carried the Irish colours creditably in several races abroad.

As for me, the Nash behaved very satisfactorily, and I was happy to make second fastest time to Torrie Large. It was quite a change to be among the award winners again.

In May the Irish Motor Racing Club held a Standing Start Half-Mile Sprint event on a by-road in the Phoenix Park, thereby bringing motor sport of a sort back to the famous venue which had not been used since that fateful year, 1939. This was an enjoyable meeting in ideal surroundings, but straight-line sprints are never very exciting. The thought went through the minds of many of us that this course, together with its return road, would make an excellent circuit for short handicap races. And sure enough, this change was made in the following season when some first-class racing in the new fashion was seen.

The sprint event under review was mainly notable for the remarkable performance of Grattan Norman and his amazing special. Grattan is one of those people who delight in building up queer motor cars, and he is also an ardent Lancia enthusiast. His latest creation seemed to be nothing more or less than a large Lancia engine with a wheel at each corner and a small slot at the front for the

Grattan Norman in his 'Lanci Bug'

driver. After a few trial runs in this machine he had regretfully decided that some form of springing was needed, so two of the wheels were given a minute degree of freedom by the use of springs taken from—of all things—a whaler's harpoon gun! On the way to this event the engine blew a gasket and steamed all its water away. Quite undismayed, Grattan Norman brought his car to the line without water, and flashed down the course with colossal acceleration, to make one of the best times of the day. I shudder to think what he must: have felt like, seated at the extreme front of this projectile at speeds in excess of 90 miles per hour, and closely pursued by a very hot and fit-to-bust engine.

Again my Frazer Nash performed with distinction, and I found my name appearing in the results with some quite satisfactory places.

It was at about this time that a new and important trophy was put up for competition among the Irish drivers. This was a beautifully executed silver model of the well-known Phoenix Monument, which stands in a prominent position by the main road in the Phoenix Park. It had originally been presented to Mr. Walter Sexton of the Royal Irish Automobile Club in recognition of his work in organising the famous series of Grand Prix races which had been run in the Park in the late twenties. On his death, Mrs. Sexton had handed back the souvenir to the R.I.A.C. with the suggestion that it should be used as a prize for motoring competitions, a gesture which was very much appreciated by our governing body.

It became known as the Walter Sexton Memorial Trophy, to be presented annually to the most successful driver in all Irish speed events. A system of marks was devised, so that honours in minor sprints and hill-climbs and more important road races would be allotted proportionately.

The effect of this new competition was to add new interest to all events run in the country, and we now had something akin to the British Gold Star for road racing or hill-climbs for which to compete.

That summer the enterprising Limerick Light Car Club decided to promote sand racing at a little resort known as Lahinch on the extreme west coast of Ireland.

With fond memories of my last venture in this rare form of the sport some 17 years before, I decided that it would be fun to take my Nash down to the West, and to combine the event with a few days' holiday and a spot of tourism. The touring equipment was duly replaced on the long-suffering car, and in company with a number of Dublin would-be contestants we drove down to this wind-swept spot on the edge of the Atlantic.

Such a thing as a motor race had never been heard of before on these wild shores, and the entire population of the West of Ireland seemed to be assembled on the sand dunes to see the fun.

As is quite usual in this type of sport, the organisers are in the uncertain hands of Mother Nature, and when the scheduled time for the start of the race arrived, the proposed course was still six inches under the Atlantic Ocean. However, the tide somewhat grudgingly receded, and after about an hour's delay the officials dashed out with their marker flags and staked out a long and very wet course.

I had intended to strip my car of its touring equipment on arrival, but when I surveyed the locks of water standing on the course I decided it would be wise to retain the mudguards. Indeed, when I saw the drenched condition of the unfortunate drivers of single-seater racing cars at the end of the first heat, I was very glad to have the protection from the flying spray and stinging sand. This heat was won by Paddy Le Fanu, in his Meadows-engined special, and he had also taken the precaution of leaving his mudguards in position.

Soon the second heat, in which I was drawn, was got going and I settled down to the task of re-learning how to drive on sand. As we sped along in a flurry of salt spray, memories of the old days at Tramore flooded back. Indeed, I was soon to be reminded forcibly of those days, and just how unsuitable a chain-driven car is for sand racing. The gear lever became stiffer and stiffer, and unpleasant grinding noises began to be audible in various parts of the transmission. But the engine continued to function well, with only an occasional splutter as we dashed through the deeper ponds of sea water which lay on the sodden course. I soon found myself in the lead, a position which I managed to hold until we received the chequered flag.

The final was a hurried affair, with the officials gazing anxiously at the tide, which, true to form, had decided to advance before its scheduled hour. I knew I could expect a good scrap with Paddy Le Fanu and, sure enough, we found ourselves in close company for a few laps. But the wet sand continued to find its way into the exposed gear mechanism of my car, and soon I found my gear lever immovably stuck in the third gear position, and Paddy's low, green car drew away and finally won this event, which became known as the 'Atlantic Grand Prix'.

In the last few laps the tide had advanced until the course had been squeezed into the shape of a banana, and cars travelling on one 'straight' were close enough to throw spray on the racers proceeding in the opposite direction on the other.

I undoubtedly enjoyed this trip to the West, but after the many hours of washing and scraping necessary to get my car clear of the clogging sand and fit to drive home, I decided that I would not be easily induced to drive in another sand race. Even to-day I can find traces of the abrasive mixture in hidden corners of the chassis.

……………………..

Early in September came the event for which I had been patiently waiting. This was to be another of the race meetings over the 'short circuit' at the Curragh.

My entry form was duly filled in, the old car was again stripped of its touring equipment, and on that bright Saturday just nine years after my last appearance in a road race, we set out for the plains of the Curragh.

I have made it a rule in these notes to avoid lengthy descriptions of races which have passed off without incident, and if I stick to this rule I must dismiss this Curragh meeting in a few words. But as, for private reasons, this was likely to be my last fling, I feel justified in letting my mind and my pen linger awhile.

On arrival in the paddock, a glance at the day's programme and the handicap allowance showed that I was quite favourably placed on the list. I think that the handicapping committee had lost track of possible performance of my Frazer Nash and, with due respect for its age, had given it a fairly generous allowance. I found that I had five seconds' start from three Northern H.R.G.s, and these cars are simply more modern editions of my Frazer Nash, with so-called 'improvements' such as normal gearboxes and the abolition of chain drive. I felt that if I could stay in front of these cars I would not have much trouble with the rest of the field.

Driving in a handicap race in this open country was a new and interesting experience. The slower cars could be seen spread out in the distance, like highly-coloured insects on the green background. As I drove I could speculate on just how much I was gaining on each car, while a glance rearward would tell me if the gap between me and the backmarkers was remaining sufficiently wide. Passing was a little tricky on the rather narrow, undulating roads, but the speeds on such a short course were hardly high enough to be dangerous. Everything depended on last-second braking for the hairpin corners and the last ounce of acceleration away from them again.

One by one the slower cars were overhauled and passed, while there seemed to be no serious threat from behind. Then suddenly I realised that there was no one in front, and I was in the Iead. On the next lap I received the chequered flag and saw the flutter of spectators' programmes in mild applause.

This win in my heat had established a place for me in the final, which would be the principal event of the afternoon. Needless to say, I gnawed my fingernails with impatience while the other heats were run off.

As I started the engine to go out to the start I noticed a new and ominous thump from under the bonnet. My eyes instinctively dropped to the oil gauge, but all seemed normal in this department. The exhaust note sounded clean and there was no undue smoke.

I was puzzled by the noise and filled with foreboding, but I just had to run in that final.

The line-up was somewhat similar to that in the previous heat, but now the scratch car was the very fast K3 supercharged Magnette of Hector Graham. This beautiful red single-seater was always impeccably turned out and the characteristic crisp exhaust note was a joy to hear. Its very special fuel left a strong aroma of 'boot-polish and pear-drops' lingering in the atmosphere.

The race was on, and I settled down to overtake the slower cars now spread out at intervals into the far distance on the undulating road. The ugly thump was still in the engine, but no worse, and the oil pressure remained normal. Brakes, however, were beginning to fade, and I found myself coming into the very acute corners with too much speed. The result was a good deal of clumsy broad-siding and the rear wheel clouting the low roadside banks, sending up showers of clay and clods of earth.

I had ten laps in which to overtake the field, and I felt sure I could do it if the engine would hold together. But my confidence was rudely shattered when Hector Graham came up behind and flashed by with an ear-splitting roar, one finger cocked from the steering wheel in cheery acknowledgment.

I was disappointed, but second place was better than nothing and I redoubled my efforts to catch the leaders, determined to let no one else go by. One by one the slower cars fell astern, until I was sure there was no other car in front except the red M.G. which had long since disappeared in the distance ahead.

Imagine my surprise and joy when, on rounding the last corner before the finish, I saw the chequered flag and my number held out to signify that I had won.

Yes, my calculations of my position on the handicap had gone wrong, and I had not realised that Hector Graham was so far back on the list that he would have had to pass me twice to take the lead.

I drove back to the paddock, full of that bubbly feeling which is only induced by a win in a motor race. As the car came to rest I received a hearty slap on the back, and I was deeply touched to receive congratulations from Ainsley Verschoyle, now well on in his eighties, who had turned out to see the car which had been his choice 15 years before, first over the line again.

The author presenting the Walter Sexton Trophy to Billy Bradshaw-winner in 1956, 58 & 59

This win was something more than a minor victory in an unimportant short-distance road race. It was the culmination of the first season in which the Walter Sexton Trophy was inaugurated.

During the summer I had picked up odd points here and there, and almost unnoticed by me, they had been steadily accumulating. With the addition of the points allotted for this race I found myself the first holder of the Trophy.

To use an American expression, I was now Champion Race Driver of the Year.

If my old Frazer Nash could speak, I think it would have asked me quietly if I didn't think it had now done enough.

Instead, it signified its thoughts more forcibly. On the way home from that Curragh race the long-suffering crankshaft turned its last revolution. It shattered itself so effectively as to make sure that nothing further could be expected from the remainder of the engine.

CHAPTER XXVIII.

Motor Sport from the Grandstand

TWO more years have gone by.

Two years of watching others compete, from the grandstand, the roadside bank, or with the privilege of an important-looking official brassard. I have seen the best drivers in the world compete before the King of England and a hundred thousand of his subjects. I have seen our own Joe Kelly showing the Irish racing colours in a full Grand Prix.

I have seen the trophy which I won at Cork pass twice in succession to the hands of Joe Flynn, who was still a schoolboy in those far-off days, and the Walter Sexton Trophy go first to Joe Kelly and then to Pierce Cahill. I have felt the heart-stopping omen of disaster as a column of black smoke rose in the distant still air signifying a serious crash, and the surge of relief as the announcer quoted: "No one injured."

These years have not been without mild participation in the humbler events. The breaker's yard yielded yet another Meadows engine for my car, and it took to the road again in many reliability trials.

At first I had thought seriously of having a try at breaking into the select band of those heading the list in the reliability trials world. The idea of having a place on the winning team for the Hewison Trophy, which is the equivalent of the British Trials Drivers Championship, certainly appealed to me. The possibility of winning the individual championship even crossed my mind.

I set to work to make the Frazer Nash more suitable for this arduous sport. The ground clearance was increased, steel undershields were fitted, gear ratios were lowered, and tyres were let down to pressures little more than atmospheric.

And after about six trials in which we were listed among the lower second-class awards or in the 'also finished' category, I sadly came to the conclusion that I was reaching for the moon.

Nevertheless, I enjoyed this last effort, and I have felt genuine pleasure on the rare occasions when my name has appeared among the award winners. I felt no shame in leaving the premier awards to such drivers of the new era as Jim Millard, Kevin Murray, Johnnie Bell and Cecil (Monte Carlo) Vard.

The return of motor spirit in comparative plenty has brought the revival of the long distance trial or 'rally' type of competition, and by taking part I have seen many parts of this island that would not be traversed in years of normal touring. The enterprising Limerick Club has run such an event as an annual holiday fixture, and through this medium I have seen glorious scenery, stark mountain passes and the accepted beauty of Killarney's lakes, with the added zest of a little mild competitive motoring to enliven the more humdrum sections of the route.

....

Twenty years have slipped by. Twenty years under the spell of motor sport, with all the disappointments, the thrills, the tension, the successes.

Many will say that it was twenty years of wasted effort. That if I had directed my energy to more important matters I might now be a man of means.

But if I had the leisure moments of those years to live again, would I use them more sensibly, usefully, or profitably?

Would I?

THE END

'Daithi' in Nash at Cruagh Hill Climb

INTRODUCTION

HAVING known the Colley family and especially my good friend Tony for the past 35 odd years, it gives me great pleasure to write a few words as an opener to Tony's addendum.

The exploits and fun we have had over the years with old cars will never be forgotten and Tony's enthusiasm is still as mustard keen as it was when I first set eyes on him and his great old brown Nash.

I have no doubt that the reader will enjoy this book as much as I have - long live all these old cars.

DAVID DUNN

CHAPTER 29

(Addendum by Tony Colley)

Chain Reaction

DUDLEY COLLEY died in 1959, 8 years after this book was published and, coincidentally, 8 years after I was born. With the unstoppable energy of Wilfie Fitzsimmons, the two of them produced "Wheel Patter" which found a place, not only in the hearts of the Irish Motor Sport enthusiasts but further afield, not least on the book shelves of members of the Frazer Nash Section of the Vintage Sports Car Club.

My brother Finlay and I grew up in a very 'automotive' atmosphere generated hugely by the friends and relations of my late father. Their tireless support for my mother at that time undoubtedly fired my own enthusiasm, as more and more stories of adventures involving motorcycles, racing specials and sportscars drew me to the conclusion that, yes, I too would like to be part of a world so colourfully illustrated in the previous chapters of this book.

My education took the form of spending formative years attending school in Dublin as a day pupil. I mention this because the upside of this arrangement was that after 3pm everyday I was free to roam the streets, or more importantly the back lanes that usually had small motor repair businesses thriving in 60's Dublin. Those garages often had old sports or racing cars lurking in dark corners, many left over from the years after World War II when they provided a competitive seat for some enthusiast. Now they were old, uncompetitive and almost valueless. We in Ireland were a little slow to recognise that there might be a future for a retrospective form of motor sport in spite of the fact that this nation was host to the Gordon Bennett Cup Race in 1903, The Ards TT from 1928 to 1936 and

International Grand Prix in Dublin's Phoenix Park, Cork and Limerick. The result was that many of these old cars were sold for a pittance or simply broken up. I recall seeing many a small trailer mounted on the rear axle of a vintage car complete with spoked wheels and traditional hub spinners.

However other nations had started to develop an interest in collecting old motor cars and many of the more desirable or interesting Irish examples were quickly snapped up. A friend who lives in Wales on the side of the main road to the port of Holyhead tells me of countless dozens of veteran and vintage cars he used to see being exported from Ireland. The exodus had begun and continued for many years.

Probably the greatest stroke of good fortune that befell Finlay and me was that my dear mother chose not to sell my father's old motor cars at the difficult time that followed his death. Bobbie Newell came to the house and put both the old Renault and the Frazer Nash up on blocks, drained the radiators and filled the cylinders with oil. Who knew when they might run again?

A 50cc Puch scooter with tiny wheels was my first road vehicle. With zero performance it provided transport to and from school and also served as my conveyance in my first job as messenger boy with an advertising agency in Dublin. The misconception then was that if you start at the bottom you most certainly end up owning the firm. However rain and boredom forced me to change both job and transport and I advanced to a side-valve 1949 Morris 8 which Finlay had bought from one Jim Boland.

Anyone who has had even the slightest passing interest in old motor cars cannot fail to have heard of Jim Boland whose knowledge and devotion to veteran cars has always had an intoxicating influence on me and many others. Veteran and vintage car rallies all over the country, often in one of Jim's wonderful lofty cars, are amongst my fondest memories. His legendary wit and generosity are renowned in motoring circles.

Motor racing in Ireland between 1958 and 1967 was confined to three road race meetings - around the roads of Dunboyne in County Meath, Rathdrum in County Wicklow, and of course the Phoenix Park. There were hill climbs and sprints and, of course, tarmac rallying was in its infancy and about to thrive. All of these I had visited as a child but in May 1968 Finlay, schoolfriend George O'Callaghan and I drove the Morris to the inaugural meeting of Mondello Park Motor Racing Circuit in Co. Kildare. Having queued forever in traffic approaching the circuit I recall peering through the chicken wire at the spectacle therein not realising that visits here were to become frequent. The programmes I collected bear testimony to the visits of yet-to-be World Champions as James Hunt, Nigel Mansell, Emerson Fittipaldi and a very young Ayrton Senna da Silva.

The following year the newly formed Sports Section of the Irish Veteran and Vintage Car Club had gathered together enough old car owners to form a grid of 'racing' cars to race at Mondello Park. This event was to hold huge significance for me as it was at this time I met John Porter and David Dunn who had entered his 1929 4.5 litre Bentley in this race. David or 'Daithi' was to become my guru, mentor and one of my closest friends. It was he and his uncontainable enthusiasm and energy that inspired me to look to my father's old Frazer Nash as means of joining him and the others for a bit of motor sport.

The 'Sports Section' grew quickly and owners of the few remaining prewar sports cars in Ireland were targeted and encouraged to restore, rebuild, even resurrect these machines for a new era of combat.

Lack of funds taught me quickly how to effect mechanical repairs on the tired old Morris 8. The novelty of a small side-valve engine powered car had worn off. An

Austin Healey 3000 with a missing first gear turned up locally and, well, I had to have it. Anyway, it was a steal! Having found a gearbox in the pages of 'Exchange and Mart' for £15 I had it sent from England to Rosslare. I was obliged to drive the Morris to Rosslare to collect it complete in a large wooden crate. Having discarded the crate I managed to get the gearbox on to the back seat of the car and head for Dublin.

On the journey the behaviour of the Morris changed. I wondered if it was resentful of my plans to replace it as it started to pull heavily to the left and towards the hedge. Turning the steering wheel to the right induced a dreadful rubbing noise. What could be broken that hadn't broken before? The cart springs that hold the front axle on that glorious model had a reputation of breaking in the middle and that reputation was maintained on this occasion. The break had caused the axle to slip backwards on one side introducing a new direction. I jacked up the car and dismantled the set of leaf springs by loosening the bolts and shoved the axle forward close to its original position, broken ends of leaf springs now meeting. Experience had taught me to always carry a 'vice grips' but, for some lucky reason, this time I had two. Having clamped the new assembly of leaf springs and axle with both I then 'borrowed' some barbed wire from a nearby hedge and wound it around the handles to ensure they wouldn't fly open. Job done, I was away and reasonably straight. I wonder if the next owner ever found my roadside repair. I never looked at it again.

The Austin Healey introduced me to the principles of a sporting car. It was small but fairly powerful having a large push-rod six cylinder engine usually found in taxis. Fitted to a sports car body it could move away very rapidly making all the right noises. The result was a very attractive package - particularly to officers of the law!

Driving around Dublin I soon met the other 3(!)

owners of big Healeys and our small fraternity was formed, essentially to swap or buy bits. I remember buying a superb hard top and a chromium plated rocker cover - the bees knees!

Some time later I was deemed to be at fault when a connection between the Healey and a family saloon in Lucan one wet Saturday afternoon dented both ego and pocket. I was forced to sell to cover the cost of repairing both cars.

A Triumph TR2 was advertised in the evening paper as an 'unwanted' engagement present (disengagement, perhaps?) for £60. My cousin Christy Hone accompanied me on many of these reconnoitres and this one found us attempting to drive the purchased item from Greystones to Clondalkin. We felt that it was wise to travel over the Dublin mountains to avoid any encounter with the law but our enthusiasm for the 'new' machine made us overlook its running condition. A loud knock from the lower deck indicated a very worn big end bearing, but what the hell - it was going to be rebuilt anyway. That warm evening in Autumn was pleasant enough for the expedition but the light disappeared rapidly introducing a cheery moon. Funny how cars can let you down miles from anywhere but the TR ground to halt about 30 yards from the Sally gap crossroads. Pushing the car into a position so the moon illuminated the engine we discovered the mechanical fuel pump had failed. Nothing for it - we both took turns sitting inside the open bonnet operating the pump by hand while the other drove with head leaning out of the window to see the road home.

Complete dismantling of the engine revealed a very undersized crankshaft so grinding it was out of the question - I had to get a replacement. That fountain of knowledge David Dunn immediately provided the answer. The same crankshaft was fitted to the old Ferguson TVO tractor of which there were still many in use or lying in hedges or ditches in the early 70's. I found such an engine in the haggart behind a tractor dealer's premises in Rathangan. Having negotiated the purchase of the engine for £15 I'll not forget the look on the man's face as I turned it upside down, pulled off the sump, removed the crankshaft.... and left.

The car's restored life was uneventful but it had a tendency to spin without any real provocation. It served as transport on my honeymoon when Mary and I drove it to live and work in Amsterdam where it gave trouble-free motoring, but was stolen once.

During those years of exploiting my interest in 50's and 60's sports cars a frustration was growing - I really wanted to understand, drive and maybe even compete my father's Frazer Nash with the now thriving Sports Section. Finlay had already started the restoration of the Nash and had it well advanced with a lot of help and advice from Bobbie Newell. At one point we exhibited it in chassis form at the "Century on Wheels" motor show in Dublin's RDS. Bodyless it was an opportunity to see the chain driven transmission in all its glory.

The fever had gripped me by now and the Sport Section had matured enough to be invited to produce a grid of 'vintage' racing cars at the International race meeting in the Phoenix Park in 1974. As a self-appointed cheerleader and general runner I accompanied David Dunn who had entered a magnificent Talbot 105 on which he had built very faithful replica team car bodywork. The race was won by Dr Brendan O'Hara driving a FIAT special originally conceived by Grattan Norman, and David finished a creditable 5th.

The following year the Nash was ready and I duly entered my first motor race in the Phoenix Park in 1975. Even then we drove without flameproof overalls and the only concession to modern times was the compulsory crash helmet. We often raced in short sleeved shirts! I finished somewhere near the back having spent the entire race carefully studying my mirror. The shock was the realisation of the pace and length of all those races my father competed in before and after the war.

Frazer Nash racing at Mondello Park in the 70's.
-photo George O'Callaghan

With the car now running in 'raceworthy' condition I entered it in virtually every event the Sport Section offered, including hillclimbs all over the country. One Enniskerry hillclimb gave me a time which was 1/4 of a second slower than my father's time on the same course in 1951. I blamed the introduction of a footpath to the course for my tardiness!

The Corkscrew hillclimb in Co. Clare beckoned a revisit and having arrived on Friday for the weekend I decided to drive the hill to familiarise myself with the course. Fellow 'vintage' racer Derek Ryan, who recently is sadly deceased and much missed, elected to accompany me on this exploratory run up the hill in the Nash. Half way up he demanded that I stop and release him insisting that he'd walk back. I guess I was beginning to learn the handling characteristics of a chain driven car with no differential.

Cruagh Hill Climb.

-photo Ronan Lee

During the 1970s the Vintage Sports Car Club were running a full calendar of race meetings in the UK and the nearest and most attractive to us in Ireland was the meeting at Oulton Park in Cheshire. David Dunn by now had acquired a 1936 Lagonda LG45 team car so we decided to enter both cars and duly headed off to the ferry from Dublin to Liverpool. I had entered a race specifically for Frazer Nash cars and felt that, being an unknown entity, I might have a chance with the handicap. Various groups of cars were flagged off with appropriate time lapses and I had counted how many were ahead of me. After what seemed an age my 'group' was released. Wheels spinning, tyre smoke, engine smoke and we were away and, yes, I seemed to have the edge. I set off in pursuit and soon gained on the cars ahead. One by one I picked them off and my poor mathematics told me that I must be leading! After another lap on the ragged edge I thought I saw the tail of another Nash disappearing round the next corner far in the distance. I had miscalculated, but soon I reeled it in and got by. If it would just keep going and if I didn't make any mistakes I might just win this.

My pace increased when, in my mirror I saw a Frazer Nash radiator creep into view. Then another, and another and another, until quite a large group were sliding around every bend behind me. One lap to go - was it possible? Around the last right-hander they were snapping at my heels. I could see the chequered flag being raised but, as we crossed the line, one on the left and two on the right passed me with three more just behind! I reckon there must have inches in it...... but I was placed fourth.

Many further visits and the wonderful hospitality of the Parkers in Chester made it an annual pilgrimage to Oulton Park. Then to Silverstone where it always seemed to rain and in 1979 I entered the Frazer Nash Raid to Bolzano. This was a mighty drive from home through England joining members of the Frazer Nash Section of the VSCC in London, heading through France, Germany, Austria into Northern Italy and the South Tyrol, covering over 3000 miles. Two glorious weeks were spent charging around the famous passes that were the course of the Alpine Trials where Frazer Nashes were victorious in the 30's.

A full calendar of events at home kept the Frazer Nash active. I returned the car to Craigantlet for a run in the 'vintage' class. I was first to practice a run up the hill on a sunny summer's evening and, having never visited the venue before, I was completely unfamiliar with the course. Briskly away I found myself charging up a new section of roadway with many parked cars ahead. Out of the corner of my eye I noticed a solitary hay bale just after a turn left. Should I have turned left there? I slowed, stopped and reversed for a closer look at the hay bale. It had attached to it a piece of paper about the size of an envelope. On it was a hand-drawn arrow indicating that, yes, I should indeed have turned left. Ahem, I guess I am possibly the only driver to have gone the wrong way up Craigantlet! The next day there was another hay bale in the middle of the main road with a very large arrow attached.

The Sports Section of the IVVCC had a variety of events including their annual navigational rally. In 1981 I wisely chose David Miller as my co-driver whose unquenchable thirst for motorsport is inspiring. A long, tough morning had us with a clean sheet by the lunch stop - in other words no points lost, thanks to his skills in the passenger seat - a rare place for him, though.

About half way through the afternoon run we made a critical error which was, of course, the fault of an inaccurate road map. An earlier driving error had us lose first gear chain. Not reckoning on needing it we pressed on to avoid losing time. However, our mistake had us driving some considerable distance on a 'white' - a very rough track which eventually led us to a 'ford' across a river which was about 18 inches deep in places with a steep entrance and exit at each side. We stopped and Dave got out to consider the best plan of attack. Not having the traction of first gear ratio we decided that I should take a run through in second gear with a little build up of speed for momentum. So I reversed a few yards for my charge and, on Dave's instruction, I floored it in second gear. Down with a huge splash into the river, the now submerged Frazer Nash with its exposed flywheel and clutch was roaring and spraying water everywhere like a paddle steamer on steroids! Alas, it ground to a halt. Nothing for it - out of the car and push. Up to my waist in the river by now and Dave ripping off his shoes and socks we managed to get it out of the water without stalling the engine. This failed amphibian attempt had cost us a lot of time so, after a brief inspection of car and crew, we set off in a great hurry. Dave's calls were flawless - 'fast left, 40, square right into.....' Two stationary tractors parked in the middle of a narrow road, the drivers chatting whilst having a fag! This was the moment I discovered that the brake drums were still full of water rendering any attempt at arresting forward motion utterly useless. Evasive action was required so I dived to the left exposing my unfortunate navigator to the ditch in favour of the cold steel of the tractor which, I should add, had a double bladed hedge trimmer at exactly eye level.

David Miller adjusts tracking after off-road excursion.

Miraculously we had not connected with anything that wasn't organic and the damage was slight - the track rod was badly bent but with suitable force and the aid of a farm gate we got it nearly right and we were off again. Sadly the time taken was excessive and we were classed as a non-finisher.

Dave's friendship over the years has often had me in the passenger's seat during competitive events and there is no other place to be to witness the 'Millerman' driving in anger to an almost certain win, irrespective of the car. The image of Dave racing his single-seater supercharged MG special at Silverstone beating ERAs in the wet or competing a Jaguar Mk. 1 in the Killarney Historic Stages Rally is something to behold.

In 1981 Daithi Dunn invited me to join him on a trip to Brookland's Society's annual meeting at the famous circuit in Surrey. He had restored his 1936 LG45 Lagonda team car. This car was built by Fox and Nicholls for the 1936 LeMans 24 hour race which was cancelled due to a rail strike. It subsequently raced very successfully, but it was particularly apt that it should return to Brooklands that year, as Alan Hess was guest of honour. For it was he who, in 1936, had driven that car for one hour and recorded over 100 miles, the first sportscar to have done so.

One of the drives during the day's event was for all cars to have a run up the famous 'Test Hill' - a very steep incline with a stop half way up. As we had been invited to some of the society's generous hospitality earlier we had missed the opportunity to view the hill before the run. A hurried arrival at the foot had us set off up the first section where we were obliged to stop momentarily before thundering up to the top. Neither of us spoke as we gained speed delivered by the stout 4.5 litre Meadows engine. All we could see ahead was a horizon indicating the brow of the hill. The image in my mind was of that famous photograph of this hill with Archie Frazer Nash in mid-air in his GN - all wheels airborn. I suddenly thought - what if, all these years later, they've built a souvenir shop at the top, or a public toilet? Mercifully our 'landing' was unimpeded despite a heavy touch-down!

Daithi's generosity over the years has allowed me to race his 4.5 litre Bentley and the Lagonda, not to mention navigating with him in the 'Jagnette' (an MG /Jaguar special) in the Killarney Historic Stages Rally where we were rewarded with two class wins.

One Oulton Park VSCC meeting had Daithi and I share the Frazer Nash. After the day's racing, friend and Nash exponent Fred Giles invited me to drive his GN special 'Beetle' around the paddock before joining him and Daithi in the circuit bar for a drink. Having enjoyed some time 'playing' with this splendid single-seater racing car, I drove it to the entrance of the bar which was a sort of pre-fab with sliding-doors at ground level. As I approached, Fred and Daithi slid open the two doors revealing a space where they had quietly moved chairs and tables aside. The temptation was too great: helped by the beckoning calls of members of the Frazer Nash Section of the VSCC. out with the clutch...... and into the centre of the bar. This move was met with great hilarity from the assembled drinkers but with less than approval from the landlord. As he bellowed in my ear to turn it off and get it out, I searched for reverse gear lever. But it wasn't in the same place as the Nash. I thought it best to switch it off now, as he threatened to close the bar and throw everyone out. Removal of the car seemed like the best plan so, as nobody could or would help me, I had to grab each rear wheel and reverse it out like a wheel chair. Some pacification was then required to calm the landlord sufficiently to keep the bar open.

In those years of active competition it was always necessary to keep the cars running as well as possible, even developing where possible, but of course replacement original parts were non-existent. The very active 'Spares' department of the Frazer Nash Section of the VSCC was a regular source of vital bits but often one had to work on the advice of learned members.

The original con-rods in the Meadows engine are made of duralium which, although being very light, becomes very brittle with age, and can snap easily if the engine is revved high enough. Most Frazer Nash owners by then had replaced the rods with steel ones. Fortunately I never suffered this calamity and, in ignorance, I had driven the car to the South Tyrol with such original rods still in the car.

Having arrived at the top of the famous Stelvio pass in 1979 I remember the look of horror on the faces of the other assembled 'raiders' when I let it slip exactly how original my engine was!

Common sense prevailed and, on my return, work commenced on building a stronger engine. Rods from a Rover 12 were sourced and countless hours and evenings were spent in Daithi Dunn's garage resulting in an engine that took merciless thrashing from 1980 until 2000.

Frazer Nash on its way to 3rd place in the Phoenix Park 2000

-photo David Miller

The now tired engine took me back again to Craigantlet, the Stormont Festival in Belfast, the Curragh and Wicklow Revival meetings. In 1998 I shared the car with Nashman Sam Stretton on the Frazer Nash Irish Raid which was a circuit of the country culminating in two races each in the Phoenix Park. At one point an oil change was necessary and, as I was draining the sump of its grey contents, a passer-by asked what type of oil I used. I could only reply: "Silk vinyl emulsion!"

I cannot finish without expressing my gratitude to Daithi Dunn who kept me 'running' through all those years, even winning the Phoenix Park handicap race and the Championship of the IVVCC Sports Section. He also built a single seater body for the car which I ran for a couple of years and which we shared at Oulton Park.

More recently he paid me the ultimate compliment inviting me to drive his 1929 4.5 litre Bentley at the 24 hour Le Mans Classic

I am very lucky to be blessed with the use of a famous Frazer Nash which has introduced me to a wonderful group of friends and many unforgetable adventures.

Whereas I am not at all wealthy, I believe I am very rich.

FRAZER NASH TT Replica Reg. No. IO 3751

1934 February 1st	Car purchased by Ainsley Verschoyle	
Bray		DNS
Phoenix Park	Fastest lap 72mph	**11th** *(70.40)*
Mount Venus Hill Climb		**6th** *(45 sec)*
A. Verschoyle		
1935		
Leinster Trophy (Bray)	Fastest lap 51.24mph	**1st** *(51.24mph)*
Tallaght	Fastest lap 63.3mph	Retired
D. McCracken		
Limerick Grand Prix	Fastest lap 61.87	Retired
M. Barrington		
1936		
Leinster Trophy (Tallaght)	Fastest lap 66.98mph	**3rd** *(60.20mph)*
M. Barrington		
Craigantlet Hillclimb	1500 u/s	**1st**
Faye Taylour		
Kilternan Hillclimb	Open Handicap	**2nd**
M. Barrington		
1937	*(D. Colley test drove Frazer Nash in March)*	
Phoenix Park GP	Fastest lap 80.7mph	**8th** *(73.8mph)*
Nash Cup		
Kilternan Hillclimb	1500cc scratch	**2nd** *(46.6 sec)*
Kilternan Hillclimb	Manifold Cup	
IMRC Turvey Ave		**7th**
DUMC&LCC Turvey Ave		**4th**
IMRC Trial	Boxing Day	**1st Class**
LMC	Motorist Night Trial	**1st Class**
1938		
IMRC Trial	St. Patrick's Day	**1st Class**
Spring Trial		**1st Class**
Nendrum Trophy		**2nd**
DUMC&LCC Night Trial		**1st Class**
Craigantlet Hill Climb		**5th FTD** *(98.0sec)*
IMRC Turvey Ave		**4th FTD**
IMRC Turvey Ave		**3rd FTD**
M. Burke		
LMC Expert's Trial		**2nd Class**
Leinster Trophy		**9th**
DUMC&LCC	Sprint Meeting	**3rd**
Kilternan Hillclimb	Manifold Cup	**3rd FTD**
IMRC Cork GP National Handicap	O'Boyle Trophy *(Timed at 95.3mph)*	**1st** *(72mph)*
Phoenix Park	Fastest lap 81.6mph	**11th** *(79mph)*
Grafton Cup Trial		**2nd Class**
IMRC Autumn Trial		**2nd Class**
Ballinascorney Hill Climb	Fastest Unsupercharged	**2nd FTD**
Ballinascorney Hill Climb		**3rd FTD**
M. Burke		
LMC October Trial		**1st Class**
1939		
LMC Leinster Trophy	Tallaght	Retired
IMRC Phoenix Park	Fastest lap 83.4mph	Retired
Kilternan Hill Climb	Scratch	**2nd**
Kilternan Hill Climb		**3rd FTD**
M. Burke		
Ballinascorney Hill Climb		**5th**
Ballinascorney Hill Climb		**4th**
M. Burke		
Night Trial		**1st Class**
IMRC Donabate	Under 1500cc	**1st**
M. Burke		

1940		
Kilternan	Unlimited Scratch	**3rd**
IMRC Turvey Ave		**2nd**
M. Burke		
IMRC Turvey Ave		**4th FTD**
LMC Trial	GVB Cup	
1946		
IMRC Turvey Ave Sprint		
IMRC Kilcroney Hillclimb	over 1100cc h/c	**1st**
IMRC Kilcroney Hillclimb	1500cc scratch	**2nd**
IMRC Kilcroney Hillclimb	Unlimited cc Scratch	**2nd**
IMRC Autumn Cup Trial		**1st Class**
IMRC Sprint	Allcomers	**1st**
1948		
Walter Sexton Memorial Trophy		**1st**
IMRC Enniskerry Hillclimb		**2nd FTD**
IMRC Enniskerry Hillclimb	1500 scratch	**1st**
DU Kilternan Hillclimb		**2nd (43.02 sec)**
IMRC Autumn Trial		**2nd Class**
IMRC Phoenix Park Sprint	Scratch	**2nd**
IMRC October Trial		**1st Class**
IMRC Curragh Races	Vigzol Trophy Sept	**1st**
LMC Leinster Trophy		
LLC&MCC Lahinch		**Winner 1st heat**
LLC&MCC Lahinch	Unlimited Scratch	**2nd**
1949		
IMRC Winter Trial		**2nd Class**
IMRC Enniskerry Hillclimb		**2nd**
DUMC&LCC Grafton Cup		**1st Class**
LMC Lincoln & Nolan Cup		
IMRC Phoenix Park Sprint	1500cc u/s scratch	**1st**
1950		
MGCCIC Experts Trial		**2nd Class**
IMRC Autumn Trial		**2nd Class**
IMRC Boxing Day Trial		**1st Class**
LMC	Lincoln & Nolan Cup	**2nd Class**
1951		
DUMC&LCC Grafton Cup		**2nd Class**
IMRC Enniskerry Hillclimb	Over 1250cc	**3rd 52.22sec**
IMRC Phoenix Park		**10th**
Dungarvan		**3rd**
1952		
CMC Curlew Hillclimb	Sligo	**1st H/C**
1956		
LMC GVB Cup Trial		**2nd**
1959 DUDLEY COLLEY DECEASED		
1962		
B.Newell		
Mount Venus	25th Anniversary	
1967		
F.Colley		
IVVCC	Sept 23/24 Wexford Rally	
LMC Veteran Car Run		
Stradbally	Aug Bank Holiday	
1975		
T.Colley		
Mondello Park	IVVCC	**Class A**